Presented to

_____

My prayer is that, as you read this book, the words on its pages will leave an indelible mark on your heart as the anointing of the Holy Spirit prepares you for our Lord's soon return.

As you adhere to the spiritual principles set forth, chapter by chapter, I believe you will be Rapture ready!

On the other hand, if you do *not* hearken to its instruction, you may be left behind when our Lord returns.

So, read carefully the Words of the Lord, knowing that the spiritual path set forth will lead you to life eternal. And, when we are all blessed to leave this old world behind in the Rapture, we will again unite as family members in Heaven and be found rejoicing together around God's throne.

By God's grace, I will meet you there!

_____   ___/___/20___

How To Be
RAPTURE
READY

McDougal & Associates
Servants of Christ and Stewards of the
Mysteries of God

How To Be
RAPTURE
READY

BY

CHARLES L. BENNETT

Published by:

McDougal & Associates
18896 Greenwell Springs RD
Greenwell Springs, LA 70739
www.thepublishedword.com

McDougal & Associates is dedicated to spreading the Gospel of the Lord Jesus Christ to as many people as possible in the shortest time possible.

ISBN 978-1-950398-41-6

Printed in the U.S., the U.K. and Australia
For Worldwide Distribution

DEDICATION

This book is dedicated to my friend, the Holy Spirit, whom I met personally in Nicaragua, Central America. When I was four and a half years old, He shined the supernatural light of God on me and imparted to me the knowledge of salvation, along with the scripture verse John 3:16, and let me know that the call of God was on my life to preach.

ACKNOWLEDGMENTS

To Annette, my wife of more than fifty years, my nine children, my twenty-six grandchildren and one great-grandchild.

To my mother, a woman of faith. While I was growing up, I heard her praying in the Spirit too many times to count while she was kneeling by her bed.

To my father, whom I always saw studying the Word in his reclining chair, digging into prophetic scriptures. He taught me so much about end-time events, especially the Day of the Lord, which is the Rapture.

To my sisters, Dianne and Kay, and my brother-in-law, Alan, who helped me edit this book. They were committed to seeing this book published.

To the multitude of ministers who have imparted into my life the Word of God.

To Harold McDougal, I could not have pulled this project together without your help.

A special acknowledgment to my son, Daniel, who financed this book from the grave through his carpet installation invention called the Seamer Down Now.

To Debbie, whom we met in Mexico when my son Daniel was there for treatments. Debbie received a miracle healing from an "incurable" disease when we encouraged her to memorize four scriptures. She has been a great source of encouragement to me while I was writing this book. Thank you, Debbie.

Contents

As it was in the days of Noe, so shall it be also in the days of the Son of Man. They did eat, they drank, they married wives, they were given in marriage, until the day that Noah entered into the ark... .

Luke 17:26-27

AUTHOR'S PREFACE

Since my earliest memories, I have been inquisitive about the "behind the scenes" of things and situations. What was on the surface did not intrigue me. It seems that God knew my desire and allowed me to come into contact with some of the key players in His Kingdom from time to time.

Once, while at the Full Gospel Businessmen's Fellowship International (FGBMFI) meeting in Washington, D.C. in the mid 1960s (when I was fifteen years old), I walked behind the curtain at a banquet and saw Demos Shakarian and Oral Roberts sitting and having a very intense conversation.

Another time, while in my twenties, I was invited to sit in on one of the business meetings of the National Religious Broadcasters (NRB) Convention in D.C. by one of their founders, Charles Leaming. Although I felt out of place, it was as if the Holy Spirit was saying to me, "I am grooming you." Little did I know that later I would be involved in radio ministry, at home and also in Central America.

I will never forget, as a young minister in my late teens, feeling led to travel two hours to meet with Pat Robertson at WYAH-TV. I was thrilled when he came to where I was and allowed me to ask him things about the ministry. That meeting with Pat Robertson may have been insignificant to him, but it was very important and powerful to me. It was significant to me because, within just a few days, I was going to be taking my first solo missionary journey to Jamaica, West Indies. It gave me increased confidence to know that, if God could direct me to meet with Pat Robertson and arrange for that meeting to take place, then God could use me and lead me throughout all parts of Jamaica. What a wonderful missionary trip that was for a nineteen-year-old who had just finished his first year of Bible college at Zion Bible Institute in East Providence, Rhode Island. I saw mighty miracles of God for forty-five days, and God opened doors and directed my steps.

Later in my ministry, I was asked by the Christian Broadcasting Network (CBN) to arrange with my friend, David Wine, who was a great missionary and tent manufacturer, to put together the T-shaped tent used in one of the most blessed outreaches in the Tidewater area for the 700 Club "Seven Days Ablaze" outreach. My large round tent of 7,200 square feet was too small to be used for the main event, but it was the perfect size to be used for their bookstore for this outreach.

All of this was only a part of the grooming of God in my life and ministry. God has a way of using all your encounters and bringing them back full circle.

I have many more stories of being with some of the greatest men of God of this past century, such as R.W. Schambach, whom I invited to come to our city of Hopewell, Virginia. Several times I was able to fly my plane to his conventions and eat ice cream with him after his meetings. Peter Youngren, Sid Roth, Mike Perky, John Bevere and Reinhard Bonnke came to our small city for the area-wide tent revivals that our church sponsored over an eight-year period of time. I also got to know Jimmy Swaggert and many other ministers, such as Rex Humbard, and many more men of God who have graced my life.

None of these encounters can be compared to the greatest encounter I have ever had in my life and ministry, which happened in Nicaragua when I personally met the Holy Spirit and I learned who He really is! He has become my Friend. Later I will tell you of this entire encounter. He is amazing. He is very real! He is everywhere all at the same time. He is also the third Person of the Godhead. He is definitely a very real person!

God has directed me to travel into many parts of the world. He has allowed me to travel to over fifty countries and has blessed me to minister to people from small groups to many thousands of people at one time! All of this has been by the grace of God.

My life has been very unusual because of the way I read the Bible and because of the supernatural encounters and experiences I have had with God! This book comes as a result of the way God speaks to me and the things He has made known to me!

Many times, over the years, I would have dreams in the night and rush to my study to research what I had dreamed. I had not known that what I just dreamed was in God's Word. Each time I have been thrilled to discover that what I had just dreamed was truly correct and accurate according to Scriptures. It is amazing to confirm that God is still communicating with mankind today. It has been thrilling to allow Him to let me look behind the scenes of His Word, and what I am about to present to you was discovered in this wonderful way.

Please understand where I am coming from. I am *not* saying that I have all the answers and that things *must* happen exactly as I describe them here. What I *am* saying is that, however things happen, you and I must be ready when Jesus comes. I believe that if you will prayerfully read through this book, the Holy Spirit will minister to you truths that you may read. But, more importantly, He can speak to your spirit what I have *not* written. Remember, the Word of God clearly states that if we are led by the Spirit, we are the sons of God. I pray that this book will help you to see *How to Be Rapture Ready.*

INTRODUCTION
MY FIRST ENCOUNTER WITH GOD

First, let me tell you how, as a boy, I came to know the Lord. My father and mother were nominal Christians who attended church regularly, but at one of the traditional denominations. Even though they each had an encounter with the Lord in their early youth and had accepted Jesus as their Lord and Savior, they were not at all "on fire" for God because they did not know that they could be led by Him on a daily basis. Their spirits were awakened, but they did not have a continuous relationship with God.

My father began to seek God as he became aware that having a wonderful wife and four children and owning his own plumbing, heating and air-conditioning business did not completely fill the inner part of his being. He began reading the Word of God to fill the void in his life. As he read the Bible, an insatiable hunger for a relationship with God came into his life, and it was as if he could not get enough of the Word of God! It was during this time that the Word also became understandable to him! While he was reading, he came across John chapter 3, where Jesus told Nicodemus that he had to be *"born again."*

About four months after this hunger for God became so prevalent in my father's life, an unusual thing happened with me that challenged my parents. Just before I turned five years of age, I had a supernatural encounter with God. I have very few memories of my life before I was five, but I can remember that a very bright light shone down on me while I was playing outside in the yard. When the bright light came upon me, the presence of God enveloped me in His love, and it was in that moment that I suddenly knew John 3:16 in its entirety: *"For God so loved the world, that he gave his only begotten Son, that whosoever believeth in him should not perish, but have everlasting life."*

I went running into the house and, with great excitement, I said to my mother, "Do you want to hear my memory verse?" That verse from scripture had been imparted to me in its entirety. My mother was flabbergasted, as she knew that the church she and my father were attending did not teach four-and five-year-old children long Bible verses, but only very short phrases that the children would repeat after the teachers, such as, *"Be ye kind one to another"* (Ephesians 4:32).

Mom was shocked, but not wanting to make a big deal out of what had just happened to me, she kept her composure and did not allow herself to overreact. She did not want to upset me! The rest of the day she pondered in her heart what had happened to me. Then, when my father came home from work, she related to him how I had come in from playing and told her about the bright light and my memory verse.

My parents' doctrinal belief at that time was that no children could be "born again" until they came to the age of accountability, which they were taught was around twelve or thirteen years of age! My father decided that my mother should go into the bedroom, where I was playing with my toys, and ask me if I had been "born again." He stood behind her, looking in from the hallway at me playing on the floor, as she asked, "Charles, are you born again?"

Feeling certain that I had never heard that phrase before, and confident that even if I had heard that phrase I would not comprehend or understand the concept of the phrase, they were both shocked when I looked up and simply said, "Yep," and continued playing with my toys.

Then my dad blurted out, "How do you know you are born again?"

They were beyond shocked when I looked back up and responded, "Because Jesus took out my hard heart and put in a soft one."

My father shared with me many times over the years that it took him several months before he came across the verses in Ezekiel that say:

And I will give them one heart, and I will put a new spirit within you; and I will take the stony heart out of their flesh, and will give them an heart of flesh.

Ezekiel 11:19

A new heart also will I give you, and a new spirit will I put within you: and I will take away the stony heart out of your flesh, and I will give you an heart of flesh.

Ezekiel 36:26

When the Holy Spirit intercepted my life before I was five years old and gave me a new heart, along with a new birth and memory verse, I had a "knowing" that I was called to preach. From that instant, I have never known a moment of my life that I did not know that God had called me, placed His hand on me and that He was always with me.

I have failed God many times and gone away, doing my own thing. I have sinned many times in my life, but I have always known that the grace of God was with me. Over the years I have learned scriptures that have kept me through the snares of life. For instance, Paul's second letter to Timothy says:

If we believe not, yet he abideth faithful: he cannot deny himself.   2 Timothy 2:13

Since God has been faithful until now in the matter of my salvation, I must believe that He will be faithful in all things, including what He has spoken about the end of time as we know it. There *will* be an end of time as we know it, Jesus *will* come again, and many of the signs of our times point to that event being very soon. Therefore, it behooves us all to be ready for it, however it happens.

The events of the end-times is one of the most divisive subjects in Christianity today. I do not wish to add to that argument. My only concern is to teach God's people not to have a closed mind concerning how the Rapture will take place. We may not instantly disappear, but no matter how it happens, we must learn *How to Be Rapture Ready.*[1]

---

1. Scattered throughout the text of this book you will find some BOOMS! I am hoping that these: 1). Will make your reading more enjoyable, and 2). Will draw your attention to concepts that may be new and, therefore, fascinating to you.

FIRST, THE END OF THE BOOK

This is the last chapter of the book. I have put it first for effect. It is only a scenario of how the events of the Rapture *might* take place. This scenario covers the greatest event of all times and includes the major concepts that Christians everywhere have referred to and have believed regarding the Rapture of the Church.

A man and his wife are in their house. It is an ordinary day, during a time when the whole world is under great pressure and change. Confusion and unrest are prevalent all over the world. There have been upheavals around the globe. It is difficult to go through daily activities because of shortages and distresses. Politicians seem to be incapable of making peace among the nations. The great nations of the world have declined in influence, and the economies of the world are in disarray. The latest nuclear exchanges between the most powerful nations of the Earth, though limited in scope, have made it clear that "peace through strength" can no longer work. The people of the whole world and the news organizations of the world seem fixated on one and only one issue: Who can make peace? Is there not *someone* who can bring peace to the world?

There is much talk about a certain politician from the Middle East who seems to have a message that could appease all groups of religious leaders, especially Muslims and Jews. He is a powerful and charismatic person, and religious leaders have announced that they would put their influence behind him so that peace can come once again on Earth.

Now, the wife speaks:

"As I was entering into the room where my husband was watching the news, I was contemplating these things and thinking that it was only last Sunday that I heard a sermon about praying that the Lord would "come quickly." While musing about this, I heard a very loud sound coming from outside my house. It sounded like a loud horn that could possibly be a new alarm system the city might have installed to alert us about problems with the local chemical plants on the other side of town. I said to my husband, 'Dear, what is that loud-sounding horn that I just heard blaring outside?' I was puzzled when he replied, 'I didn't hear any loud sound. What are you talking about?'

"Before I could respond to my husband, a man suddenly appeared in the room before me. I was overwhelmed by a knowing that he was an angel. I was puzzled in my mind, as he greeted me by my name. Amazingly, my husband apparently could not see him. This being that appeared to me began to say, 'Be not afraid. I have come to take you to a certain church where the Rapture is taking place.'

"It was then I remembered that the Bible says to *'try the spirits'*; to see if they are of God. I blurted out, 'Did Jesus Christ come in the flesh?' At the same moment I was hearing the angel's response, I heard my husband ask, 'Who are you talking to, dear? Are you crazy?' It seemed like my husband was far away in the background, but I heard the angel clearly saying, 'Of course, Jesus Christ came in the flesh. Now, let's go!'

"At that moment, I remembered hearing about a minister from the East Coast of the United States talking about how the Rapture was always called, 'The Day of the Lord,' not a 'poofing out of the Earth.' I also remembered the minister saying that Jesus warned us, *"Remember Lot's wife"* and that the Rapture could be the biggest test of a person's faith. He mentioned that the angels came and took Lot's family (including his wife) out of the city of Sodom. I remembered that pastor also saying that Jesus said, *'If you are in the field, do not go back to your house.'* The pastor also said, 'When the angel comes to take you to the place of the Rapture,

27

you should not hesitate. Nor should you delay going with the angel because you may want to check on your children to make sure they are saved. If you delay, the angel will say, 'Do as you will; I have to go now.'

"I turned to my husband and said to him, 'An angel has appeared in the room and told me I must go with him now to a certain local church because the Rapture is taking place.' My husband's impassioned response was, 'I forbid you to go with whomever you say has appeared to you!'

"Again, I remembered the pastor's sermon in which he said that the Rapture might be the greatest test of a Christians' faith. He had emphasized Luke 17, which states, '*If you are on the top of your house, do not go back down into your house. If you are in the field, do not go back to your house. One shall be taken, the other left.*' He said, 'On the day of the Rapture, do not delay trying to check on your children or loved ones. Go immediately with the angel of the Lord! Do not let anything hinder you.' He had talked about the part of Luke 17 that tsays, '*Remember Lot's wife.*'

"As I was leaving through the door with the angel, I blurted out to my husband, 'I have been a good wife to you all these years, but this time I must leave because I am not going to miss out on the Rapture.' For a fleeting moment, I thought that my husband would try to follow me to the church where the angel was taking me.

"As I was stepping off the front porch of my house, an amazing thing happened. It was as if my spirit and soul were in overdrive. My mind seemed to be unlocked, and I was able to clearly process details faster than the speed of light. I had been translated, and instantly the angel and I were at the church more than five miles away. I was puzzled because, in a fraction of a second, I had traveled more than five miles.

"Descending from above the church to the entrance, I saw what appeared to be people lying on the ground as if they were dead. It was not like me, but I was not afraid. I was at perfect peace that this was all part of the Rapture. Being filled with confidence, yet overwhelmed by my new-found ability to process the magnitude of information in microseconds, I found myself at the entrance of the church.

"As I stepped inside the church, I saw more than a thousand people sitting there. At the front of this great church, I saw what I instinctively knew was a large angel dressed like a man. He was standing behind the podium with a large book in front of him. I became aware of a conversation the angel in charge was having with a man sitting just a few rows behind me. I heard the angel saying, 'Why are you here without your robe of righteousness on?' The man did not answer for a period of time. He seemed speechless. Then the angel in charge said to the ushers, *'Bind him hand and foot, and take him away, and cast him into outer darkness; there shall be weeping and gnashing of teeth.'* Somehow, without knowing how, I knew the reference was from Matthew 22:1-14, which is The Parable of the Gathering. It was then that I understood where some of the bodies outside had come from and that the people lying there were indeed dead.

"I remembered the pastor preaching that Jesus said, *'One shall be taken and the other left.'* The disciples asked Him in Luke 17:37, *'Where, Lord?'* His response has almost never been understood nor addressed by pastors. Jesus answered, *'Where the dead bodies are, there will the eagles be gathered'* (My paraphrase). Supernaturally, I had a complete understanding of this verse, and I became aware that, during the Rapture, many will overhear what is happening and seek to push themselves into the event without being invited. The judgement of God will fall on them, and they will be slain on the spot.

"It was then that I saw the pastor of the church come through the side door. He asked the angel in charge, 'What is going on?' The angel calmly, but sternly told the pastor that he should take a seat, as the Rapture was taking place. The pastor seemed to be bewildered. He asked the angel what gave him the right to take over this church? The angel in charge simply informed the pastor that on May 8, 1958, the church members, along with the pastor at that time, had dedicated the property and the buildings to the Lord Jesus

Christ. The angel explained that the Lord Himself had now authorized this place as one of many locations that would be used as Rapture points. With that being settled, the angel in charge continued.

"I sat there in amazement as the angel called out people seated in the auditorium one by one. Then I saw the angel point at me, and I heard him ask, 'What is your name?' In fear and trembling, I answered him and told him my name. Instantly, the leaves of the book in front of him began to turn, as if by unseen hands. The angel spoke in a strong voice that could be heard all over the auditorium. It sounded as if it had been amplified, but the PA system was not turned on. He replied to me, 'Yes, your name is in the book. Come forward, up the steps to the platform.' Enveloped in the awesome presence of the Lord, I approached the angel. As I walked up the steps to the top of the platform, I noticed that every fiber of my being had begun to vibrate. When I reached the top of the steps, the angel lifted his right arm, fully extended, and said, 'Well done! Enter into the joy of the Lord!'

"As I walked under his extended arm, I noticed that I was walking about a foot above the platform. A brilliant light was shining out from my body. Then, to my shock, my body began to change in a moment, in the twinkling of an eye. My clothes were falling to the platform, but my nakedness could not be seen. I was clothed in the glory of God. It happened so fast that I could barely comprehend all that was taking place.

"When I looked up, the back of the church appeared to be open, even though I knew it was enclosed in the building structure. My supernatural eyes had been opened, and I could see through the wall. Beyond the wall there was a large chariot full of people who, like me, had been changed. They were rejoicing, crying out for joy and shouting praises to God in such a glorious and beautiful way and with a volume I had never heard on Earth before.

"I started rejoicing with them and ran on air through that back wall so fast, knowing that I had been taken by an angel to the gathering place. There I had been changed and was on my way to be carried to Heaven in a magnificent chariot, just like Elijah.

As I was getting into the chariot, I glanced over to my right and noticed the husband of my earthly life was one of those lying on the ground. He must have driven to the church to get me, but that fleeting thought could not dampen my joy. I had made it into the chariot, and I was going to my true home in Heaven, to be with my Lord."

Wow! You have just read the last chapter of the book. Now, you can continue and read all the events that have brought us to this moment. Everything in this scenario is exactly what has been taught about the Rapture over the past hundred years. The only thing different is the sequence of events. The trumpet *will* sound, one *shall* be taken and the other left, we *will* be gathered together, we *will* be changed in a split second of time, and we *will* be caught up to Heaven. This scenario may not be exactly how everything happens, but one thing is sure: Christ's coming will be sudden, and we must be ready—no matter how it happens—to make sure that we do not miss it.

If we have predetermined mind-sets as to how the Rapture will take place, we might resist the actual way Jesus comes and miss the greatest event of all ages. Reading this book will bring you into an understanding of how the Rapture *might* take place and help you to know *How to Be Rapture Ready*!

CHAPTER 2

HOW IMPORTANT IS IT THAT WE BELIEVE IN A LITERAL RAPTURE?

When Jesus asked the question, *"When the Son of Man returneth shall he find faith?"* (Luke 18:8), He was not asking it in a general sense. He was asking this in direct reference to His coming. Will He find faith in reference to the Rapture and His coming in the clouds of glory?

On Friday morning, January 22, 2021, I had a supernatural encounter. Around 4:00 AM, I was caught up in the Spirit and heard and saw a group of people discussing the Rapture of the Church. Someone in the group was saying, "We don't really have to believe in a literal Rapture because it is a take-it-or-leave-it doctrine. It is not necessary for our salvation." I saw myself saying, in this vision, that the Rapture is not a take-it-or-leave-it doctrine, but it *is* absolutely necessary for us to believe in the Rapture.

I was saying that believing in the Rapture goes directly to the point of our salvation because to *not* believe in the Rapture denies the very essence of the Gospel. Jesus Christ's birth, His life, His crucifixion, His burial, His resurrection, His ascension and His coming again are all necessary parts of our salvation. To deny His ascension is to deny His resurrection. To deny His ascension is to deny His return. The two angels that appeared to the disciples at His ascension said to them (and to us by extension):

This same Jesus which is taken from you into heaven shall so come in like manner as ye have seen him go into heaven. Acts 1:11

BOOM!

I heard myself saying in the vision that to *not* believe in the Rapture is dangerous because He is coming for those who are looking for Him and who love His appearing. We are supposed to be crying out day and night, "O Lord, come quickly!" (see Revelation 22:20). The Rapture is to be our *"blessed hope"* (Titus 2:13), and we are to comfort one another with words about our catching away (see 1 Thessalonians 4:13-18).

It seemed that in my vision I became aware of the fact that God needs our faith to draw on Heaven in order for the Lord to return. Maybe we will need some persecution before His return to shake us out of our complacency. Remember, there were four hundred silent years after Malachi before Christ was born as a babe in Bethlehem. After Malachi, there was no other significant prophet until Christ. At the end of the four hundred silent years, the situation was very similar to today. Very few of the Jews then living believed that Messiah was coming.

What about today? Will our Lord find faith when He comes? Will He find faith in you? Will you have learned *How to Be Rapture Ready?*

HUMAN DNA
THROUGHOUT THE BIBLE

You owe it to yourself to read carefully the following scriptures and let them bring faith into your spirit that God is with you at all times. No matter how much you fail Him, He is always wooing you back to Himself. For example, take consolation in the following passage of scripture from Psalm 139, and never quit serving the only true Lover of your soul, a God who in His wisdom put into the Scriptures concepts that would not be understood for centuries after they had been penned:

O LORD, thou hast searched me, and known me.
Thou knowest my downsitting and mine uprising, thou
understandest my thought afar off.
Thou compassest my path and my lying down, and art
acquainted with all my ways.

For there is not a word in my tongue, but, lo, O Lord, thou knowest it altogether.

Thou hast beset me behind and before, and laid thine hand upon me.

Such knowledge is too wonderful for me; it is high, I cannot attain unto it.

Whither shall I go from thy spirit? or whither shall I flee from thy presence?

If I ascend up into heaven, thou art there: if I make my bed in hell, behold, thou art there.

If I take the wings of the morning, and dwell in the uttermost parts of the sea;

Even there shall thy hand lead me, and thy right hand shall hold me.

If I say, Surely the darkness shall cover me; even the night shall be light about me.

Yea, the darkness hideth not from thee; but the night shineth as the day: the darkness and the light are both alike to thee.   Psalm 139:1-12

Notice the next five verses:

For thou hast possessed my reins: thou hast covered me in my mother's womb.

I will praise thee; for I am fearfully and wonderfully made: marvellous are thy works; and that my soul knoweth right well.

My substance was not hid from thee, when I was made in secret, and curiously wrought in the lowest parts of the earth.

Thine eyes did see my substance, yet being unperfect; and in thy book all my members were written, which in continuance were fashioned, when as yet there was none of them.

How precious also are thy thoughts unto me, O God! how great is the sum of them! Psalm 139:13-17

Notice particularly verse 16: *"...and in thy book all my members were written, which in continuance were fashioned, when as yet there was none of them."* The wording found here is pure inspiration from God. Scientifically, this wording could not be more perfect, even though knowledge of human Deoxyribonucleic Acid (DNA) would not be discovered for more than a thousand years. In every cell of our bodies is written every facet of our physical being. It is said that in our DNA is written the *codon* of life! Every cell of your body has the same identical strand of DNA, which, if stretched out in a long line, would be approximately twenty to twenty-two feet long. It is like a complex Morse Code that, if fully read, would take numerous volumes of books to translate.

Man was created by God, formed from the dust of the Earth and made in His image and likeness. He was the crowning achievement of all of God's creation, with the ability to procreate. He was definitely not just another life form, but a unique human being that had body, soul and spirit.

Man's ability to procreate and God's command for him to procreate would produce offspring that were far greater than the angels. God's desire and will was that man would come into his potential and ability to one day rule and reign with His Son Jesus Christ!

From a scientific point of view, all living organisms have the codon of life which, again, has come to be known as DNA. From plant life to humankind, every living thing has DNA in every physical cell.

Rhesus monkey genomes reveal DNA similarities with chimpanzees and humans. Scientists have decoded the genome of the rhesus macaque monkey and compared it with the genomes of humans and their closest living relatives—the chimpanzees—revealing that the three primate species share about ninety-three percent of the same DNA.

I do not desire to get bogged down here in scientific research, but I would like to point out that human beings have forty-six chromosomes, and the Rhesus monkey and apes have forty-eight. It is also interesting to note that there are several other animals that also have forty-six chromosomes, such as the sable antelope and Reeves's muntjac. I must also state here that the number of chromosomes does not determine how an animal looks, but the arrangement of the specific genomes on each line of the ladder of the DNA determines whether we are human or some kind of animal.

So, what is it that makes us more than physical human beings? Clearly, it is not just having a certain number of chromosomes. We, unlike other creatures, are made in the very likeness of God. We have a body, a soul and a spirit. In the next chapter, we will see how the spirit of man distinguishes him from all other aspects of God's creation. And remember, our focus in all of this is *How to Be Rapture Ready*.

CHAPTER 4

THE SPIRIT OF MAN DISTINGUISHES HIM

The spirit is a unique factor that must always be considered in this discussion. I call it "the spirit factor." God made man in His own image and likeness. He made man as body, soul and spirit. What makes human beings different from animals is this spirit factor. Man's spirit gives him intelligence that can be seen in the light in his eyes. The Word of God says:

The light of the body is the eye: therefore when thine eye is single, thy whole body also is full of light; but when thine eye is evil, thy body also is full of darkness. Take heed therefore that the light which is in thee be not darkness. If thy whole body therefore be full of light, having no part dark, the whole shall be full of light, as when the bright shining of a candle doth give thee light. Luke 11:34-36

The spirit factor cannot be seen in the DNA, chromosomes or genes, but the makeup of the structure of the DNA in the human skin allows it to resonate and reflect the glory of God. The skin of no other animal on Earth has this capability. Animals have body and soul, but no spirit. Therefore, man is not an animal!

The Word says, in reference to man's death:

Then shall the dust return to the earth as it was: and the spirit shall return unto God who gave it.
                                                    Ecclesiastes 12:7

A human being is a living soul, and we live in a body.

The Bible says of Jesus:

That was the true Light, which lighteth every man that cometh into the world.   John 1:9

At death, a redeemed man's soul and spirit goes to Heaven. Our spirit is the part of us that knows God. Many preachers have said: "Every man has a God-sized hole in his life." I take issue with those who preach that man is a spirit, he lives in a body, and he has a soul. We are living souls who live in a body, and we have a spirit. Our spirit is the part of us that knows God. It is written:

The spirit of man is the candle of the LORD, searching all the inward parts of the belly!   Proverbs 20:27

The word for *belly* in the Hebrew could be translated as "rooms or chambers of the heart." Notice what Jesus said in Matthew 6:23:

But if thine eye be evil, thy whole body shall be full of darkness. If therefore the light that is in thee be darkness, how great is that darkness!

And notice Luke 11:36:

If thy whole body therefore be full of light, having no part dark, the whole shall be full of light, as when the bright shining of a candle doth give thee light.

I believe that when Adam and Eve sinned in the garden of Eden, the light of God within them was turned off. Until then, their whole being radiated the glory of God. No man could see their nakedness because they were wearing the light of the glory of God, the same as when Moses came down from the mountain having been in the presence of God. No man could look on him that day because his skin was radiating the glory of God—the same garment made of the glory of God we will be wearing when we are changed in a moment, in the twinkling of an eye.

When the human heart is converted, the light of God is turned back on in our hearts, and when we spend time in His presence, our countenance begins to glow with His glory!

BOOM!

When the gift of the discerning of spirits was turned on in my heart, I noticed that many Christians' eyes were clear, but other Christians' eyes had parts of them that were partially dark. I did not understand this difference until the Holy Spirit taught me these scriptures. I believe that the ministers who do not understand these two scriptures are not aware that you can be a Christian and still need deliverance in the areas of your life (or rooms in your heart) that are not fully consecrated to the Lordship of Jesus Christ.

Let me state here that if a human being dies and does not know Jesus, his soul will go to Hell, but the part of him that knew God (his spirit) will go back to God who gave it. The most precious part of mankind is the part of him that knows God.

Before Satan was cast out of Heaven, he was perfect in all his ways ... until iniquity was found in him. Being lifted up in pride, he said, *"I will ascend on high; I will make my throne above God's throne, I will be like God"* (see Isaiah 14:13-14). But Satan could never be like God because he was not given free will and free choice. Even though he was a very highly intelligent being, Satan was not made with a body, soul and spirit. He has only body and soul.

The most important distinction was the fact that Satan fell without being tempted. When he fell, God could then make man in His image after His likeness with free will and free choice. Satan was the tempter. To the horror of Satan, he watched as God stooped down and began to mold man out of the clay of the Earth in His image and after His likeness.

However, when God lovingly began to scoop up this new being and to breathe into his clay-formed mouth, and the clay began to change into flesh, Satan realized that this was not exactly the way all of the created angels had been produced in times past. There was something different about this new creation. There was something special about the way God was showing honor, love and respect to this new man. Very quickly it became evident to Satan that the responsibilities and privileges given to this new man, whom God called Adam, (such as the task of naming all the animals) made him everything Satan had wanted to be but was not. Man was like God—body, soul and spirit.

The final affront to Satan came a few Earth days later when God lovingly put man to sleep and began to re-make him in the area around his ribs and around the seat of his soul and fashioned from him a second being. In this way, God made a partner and a companion for man. This must have filled Satan with rage, knowing that all angels were made in the image of males, and God had never made a mate for them. It is easy to see why Satan hates the family unit. God was designing a companion specifically for this new man that He so dearly loved! **BOOM!**

In all of this, don't forget our subject. This book is not for the purpose of creating another argument to further divide Christendom. It is to show you *How to Be Rapture Ready.*

CHAPTER 5

WHAT REALLY HAPPENED
IN THE FALL OF MAN?

Satan lost no time in scheming to disrupt the relationship God had with these two new perfect creations. Knowing how important order is to God, Satan set out to position himself at the only point on the entire Earth where Adam and Eve could disobey God. He lay in wait at the tree of the knowledge of good and evil, intending to circumvent the chain of responsibility that God had set up from the beginning.

The New Testament says that Adam was made first. Woman was formed and fashioned to be man's completer, helpmate, nurturer and lover. She was everything he needed to feel fulfilled as the man chosen, formed and fashioned by God, to keep the most beautiful garden on the Earth. God had made it just for the two of them.

As the story unfolds, Adam and Eve came to the only tree of which they were not allowed to partake.

It was then that Satan spoke directly to Eve (instead of to Adam). The sad thing is that it worked. Satan, who was the most subtle of all of God's creation, had successfully bypassed the chain of responsibility set forth by God, and he did it just by addressing Eve directly.

When Eve was thus confronted, Adam did not protect her, and she did not defer to him. There is no doubt in my mind that, as she was talking to Satan, she was glancing over at Adam. She could see that he was just as interested in the forbidden fruit as she was.

If Adam had stopped this exchange, even after Eve had eaten of the forbidden fruit, he could have redeemed her. But the moment they both partook of that fruit, all of mankind had the light of God put out in them. This must have happened before they had any children. If they had children before they ate of the forbidden fruit, then one of their children could have died for this sin. Otherwise, their children would have been born sinless. **BOOM!**

God had said, "The day you eat of the forbidden fruit, you will surely die." They did not die physically that day, but they did die spiritually.

God said that Satan was the most subtle of all of the creations, but he was not very subtle about what he said. He literally called God a liar. Read it for yourself:

And the serpent said unto the woman, Ye shall not surely die: for God doth know that in the day ye eat thereof, then your eyes shall be opened, and ye shall be as gods, knowing good and evil.   Genesis 3:4-5

Eve ate the fruit and gave it to her husband who was with her, and he also ate it. The subtlety was not in what Satan said; it was who he said it to. The New testament says that the woman was tricked, but the man was purposely in rebellion.

Paul wrote in 1 Timothy 2:14:

And Adam was not deceived, but the woman being deceived was in the transgression.

BOOM!

Man committed high treason against God. He was there right next to Eve, and yet he failed to interrupt the exchange between her and the devil. Regardless, in Genesis 3, where God placed blame on Satan, He said to him:

Because thou hast done this, ... I will put enmity between thee and the woman, and between thy seed and her seed; it shall bruise thy head, and thou shalt bruise his heel.   Genesis 3:14-15

What did God mean by the "seed" of the woman? A woman has no seed. She only has eggs. The egg of a woman has twenty-tree chromosomes, and the sperm of the man has twenty-three chromosomes, making up the forty-six chromosomes of mankind between them. What an unusual statement God made to Satan! Many theologians seem not to be aware of the fact that God had to put a fertilized egg into Mary. He fashioned both the egg and the sperm, joined them, and placed them together into her womb.

If God had used Mary's egg, Jesus would have been born in sin, just like all other children who came after Adam. Twenty-three chromosomes of the blood of Jesus would have been from Mary, and Jesus' blood would have been tainted with her sin. Thank God the blood of Jesus was one hundred percent from His Father God.

God placed within the womb of Mary a fertilized egg. The egg and sperm were both from God. This was the world's first in vitro fertilization, and it was performed when the Holy Spirit overshadowed Mary. That is why God said the Seed of the woman would bruise Satan's head. It was the Seed (Jesus) that God gave through the woman.

Wherefore when he cometh into the world, he saith, Sacrifice and offering thou wouldest not, but a body hast thou prepared me. ... Lo, I come (in the volume of the book it is written of me), to do thy will, O God. Hebrews 10:5 and 7

Hearken to the words of the angel, when he informed Mary that she would bear Jesus:

And the angel answered and said unto her, The Holy Ghost shall come upon thee, and the power of the Highest shall overshadow thee: therefore also that holy thing *which shall be born of thee shall be called the Son of God.* Luke 1:35

There He was—all God and yet all man! Thus, the Word had become flesh and began to dwell among us.

God does not place blame on woman. He assigns her difficulties, but not blame. He never said, "Because" to the woman. On the man, He does place blame:

Because thou hast hearkened unto the voice of thy wife, and hast eaten of the tree, of which I commanded thee, saying, Thou shalt not eat of it: cursed is the ground for thy sake; in sorrow shalt thou eat of it all the days of thy life; thorns also and thistles shall it bring forth to thee; and thou shalt eat the herb of the field; in the sweat of thy face shalt thou eat bread, till thou return unto the ground; for out of it wast thou taken: for dust thou art, and unto dust shalt thou return. Genesis 3:17-19

Notice, in essence, God was saying to Adam, "You did not keep your place of responsibility. Instead, you submitted to the voice of your wife." I could occupy many pages sharing on this matter of man's abdication of the chain of responsibility, but what I am trying to do here is bring you to what I believe to be the most important end-time biblical truth. It is one that I believe has only been unsealed recently. The truth I discuss in the next chapter reveals Satan's threat against the DNA of humankind. God told Satan that the Seed of the woman would bruise his head. Just three chapters later, Satan had already implemented a plan to destroy the Seed of the woman, and his goal was to destroy the DNA of mankind. The battle of the ages was set in motion.

As we delve into this next truth, keep in mind the purpose of this book, to show men and women everywhere *How to Be Rapture Ready.*

CHAPTER 6

THE BATTLE OF THE AGES
PROTECTING THE DNA OF MANKIND

Satan immediately went to work influencing his fallen angels to intermarry with the women of the Earth. Notice how quickly the DNA of mankind was tainted:

And it came to pass, when men began to multiply on the face of the earth, and daughters were born unto them, that the sons of God saw the daughters of men that they were fair; and they took them wives of all which they chose. And the LORD said, My spirit shall not always strive with man, for that he also is flesh: yet his days shall be a hundred and twenty years.
There were giants in the earth in those days; and also after that, when the sons of God came in unto the daughters of men, and they bare children to them, the same became mighty men which were of old, men of renown.

And God saw that the wickedness of man was great in the earth, and that every imagination of the thoughts of his heart was only evil continually. And it repented the LORD that he had made man on the earth, and it grieved him at his heart. And the LORD said, I will destroy man whom I have created from the face of the earth; both man, and beast, and the creeping thing, and the fowls of the air; for it repenteth me that I have made them. But Noah found grace in the eyes of the LORD. These are the generations of Noah: Noah was a just man and perfect in his generations, and Noah walked with God. Genesis 6:1-9

What could have happened to mankind that: *"God saw that the wickedness of man was great in the earth, and that **every imagination of the thoughts of his heart was only evil continually"*** (verse 5)? Satan had figured out that if he did not want the Seed of the woman to bruise his head, he would have to taint the Seed of the woman. The fact that God said of man: *"**every imagination of the thoughts of his heart was only evil continually"*** is a sign that man's DNA had somehow been changed!

If I were to line up a thousand people anywhere on planet Earth today, there would surely be no more than five to ten percent of them whose every imagination was evil continually. Most men on this planet are not *totally* motivated by evil. Something must have happened to cause the entire Earth to come to such a depraved state of mind that the whole of mankind had to be destroyed. This was a supernatural takeover of man's DNA by Satan!

Notice again verse 8, where the Scriptures record: *"But Noah found grace in the eyes of the LORD."* Why did Noah find grace in the eyes of the Lord? Because he was *"perfect in his generations"* (verse 9). But what does that mean? No one can be *perfect* in all of their generations. It doesn't make sense. It's not logical. Maybe a man could be perfect in one generation, but not in many generations. I may live to be eighty, but I am from the generation of the 1950s. A generation, in the Bible, is forty to fifty years.

That word *perfect* has the connotation and definition of being "whole" or "pure." So, the Bible is saying that Noah was pure in all his generations. In other words, God chose him, not only because he was a good man (just or fair), but most of all, because the lineage of his DNA had not been tainted by the intermarrying of the fallen angels into the human race. His DNA was pure all the way back to Adam.

The Word of God says, in Jude 1:6:

And the angels which kept not their first estate, but left their own habitation, he hath reserved in everlasting chains under darkness unto the judgment of the great day.

Noah was one hundred percent human being, not half human and half spirit.

As noted, Satan was clearly trying to mess up the DNA of mankind, to keep the Seed of the woman from bruising his head. And he almost got it done! Only eight survived the flood.

BOOM!

Was God a mean monster, or did He have to purge almost all flesh from the Earth to secure the human race, so that He could bring the Seed of the woman to Earth for the salvation of all mankind?

Were there other humans who were living on the Earth who had pure DNA going back to Adam? It's possible. Peter wrote to the churches:

For Christ also hath once suffered for sins, the just for the unjust, that he might bring us to God, being put to death in the flesh, but quickened by the Spirit: by which also he went and preached unto the spirits in prison; which sometime were disobedient, when once the longsuffering of God waited in the days of Noah, while the ark was a preparing, wherein few, that is, eight souls were saved by water.   1 Peter 3:18-20

It may be that there were many other souls with pure DNA all the way back to Adam who did not get into Noah's ark and might have repented when the flood waters began to rise. As the waters kept rising, they may have been crying out to God, sacrificing animals or anything else that might save them. Christ may have preached to them when He went down into the heart of the Earth during the three days and nights after His death.

We must remember that the Law had not yet been given, and man was living in the Age of Conscience. Only Noah found grace in the eyes of the Lord and was saved by the water of the flood, but many others might not have heard the message of the ark. This would explain why Jesus preached to those spirits who died in the flood and gave them the opportunity to accept the forgiveness of God. This would not be giving them a second chance to repent, only the opportunity to accept God's forgiveness after they had already repented.

Most Christians today do not understand that there is more to salvation than repentance. There must also be a moment when you accept your forgiveness and assurance of salvation by faith.

BOOM!

Noah didn't just get into the ark and sail it right into Heaven. He was spared death to save the human race from destruction, so that God could preserve mankind to bring the Seed of the woman (our Messiah) to Earth.

In the process, Satan's plan to destroy the human creation and the Seed of the woman from the Earth was derailed, and God began to look for a man with whom He could make a covenant, with the goal of bringing the Seed of the woman into the Earth.

Thus, began another exciting chapter of the story of mankind. Why are we interested in all of this? Because it all has to do with our salvation and our ability to serve God. Most of all, because of the day we live in, we are interested in *How to Be Rapture Ready*.

CHAPTER 7

ENTER ABRAHAM

Enter Abraham. Although he came from an idol-making city, his DNA was totally pure all the way back to Adam. God told Abraham that his seed would be like the sands of the seashore and as the stars of Heaven. He also told him that in his seed all the nations of the Earth would be blessed.

As we have seen, God needed to cut a covenant with a man so that man could bring His Seed into the Earth. God had no blood in the Earth to use when cutting this covenant, so He told Abraham:

Take me an heifer of three years old, and a she goat of three years old, and a ram of three years old, and a turtledove, and a young pigeon.   Genesis 15:9

When the Seed of the woman came, He (Christ) could then cut a new covenant for both God and man through the shedding if His own blood.

And he said unto him, I am the Lord that brought thee out of Ur of the Chaldees, to give thee this land to inherit it.

And he said, Lord God, whereby shall I know that I shall inherit it?

And he said unto him, Take me a heifer of three years old, and a goat of three years old, and a ram of three years old, and a turtledove, and a young pigeon.

And he took unto him all these, and divided them in the midst, and laid each piece one against another: but the birds divided he not. And when the fowls came down upon the carcases, Abram drove them away.

And when the sun was going down, a deep sleep fell upon Abram; and, lo, an horror of great darkness fell upon him.   Genesis 15:7-17

Next, we see, in Genesis 15, an all-encompassing prophecy that covered the next four hundred years of time. It was one of the most important prophecies in the Word of God:

And he said unto Abram, know of a surety that thy seed shall be a stranger in a land that is not theirs, and shall serve them; and they shall afflict them four hundred years; and also that nation, whom they shall serve, will I judge: and afterward shall they come out with great substance. And thou shalt go to thy fathers in peace; thou shalt be buried in a good old age. But in the fourth generation they shall come hither again: for the iniquity of the Amorites is not yet full.

And it came to pass, that, when the sun went down, and it was dark, behold a smoking furnace, and a burning lamp that passed between those pieces.   Genesis 15:13-17

Notice that God not only identified the covenant He was making with Abraham, but He also clarified and recorded the title deed of the land He was giving to Abraham's seed. At the same time, we have the amazing foretelling of who Abraham's descendants would have to fight to gain their inheritance. God knew of several classes of giants that the children of Israel would have to eradicate from the Land of Promise, and He was faithful to lay out what would happen over the next four hundred years.

In the same day the LORD made a <u>covenant</u> with Abram, saying, Unto thy seed have I given this land, from the river of Egypt unto the great river, the river Euphrates: the Kenites, and the Kenizzites, and the Kadmonites, and the Hittites, and the Perizzites, and the <u>Rephaims,</u> and the Amorites, and the Canaanites, and the Girgashites, and the Jebusites.

Genesis 15:18-21

I must interject here that in order to understand this scripture, we must understand who these "ites" really were. The word *raphaim* comes from something that happened in Noah's day. That, again, was when fallen angels intermarried into the human race:

They are dead, they shall not live; they are deceased, they shall not rise: therefore hast thou visited and destroyed them, and made all their memory to perish.

Isaiah 26:14

The word *deceased* in the *Strong's Concordance* is the number H-7496, which is the word *rapha*. The *Strong's* footnote talks about this reference referring to the Canaanites and the Raphaims. The Raphaims were beings from the same type of union as in Genesis 6. Fallen angels were intermarrying with the daughters of men. Isaiah says of the Raphaim, *"They shall not rise."*

BOOM!

In other words, there is no resurrection for them.

God cut the covenant with Abraham. He then told Abraham that his descendants would be in captivity for four hundred years and that they would come out of that captivity with great wealth. God also showed Abraham the boundaries of the land that He was giving him and his people.

Satan heard and understood that the new borders of the contest would be a much smaller area. Instead of the whole world, Satan could now focus on a much smaller area. Satan also understood that he had four hundred years in which to "mess with" the DNA in that land area. Originally, Satan did not know where the Seed of the woman that would bruise his head would come from.

God groomed Abraham for something like eighty years. He was bringing him to a place of total faith and trust because of the exchange He would need to have with this man, with whom he needed to be in covenant.

Being in covenant means that everything I have is yours, and everything you have is mine. A covenant cannot be made unless there is the cutting of the flesh and the exchange of blood. When it came time for Abraham to perform his part of the covenant, God demanded blood from him from the most sensitive part of his body. Thus, Abraham and all the males of his household had to be circumcised:

This is my covenant, which ye shall keep, between me and you and thy seed after thee; Every man child among you shall be circumcised. And ye shall circumcise the flesh of your foreskin; and it shall be a token of the covenant betwixt me and you. And he that is eight days old shall be circumcised among you, every man child in your generations, he that is born in the house, or bought with money of any stranger, which is not of thy seed. He that is born in thy house, and he that is bought with thy money, must needs be circumcised:

and my covenant shall be in your flesh for an everlasting covenant. And the uncircumcised man child whose flesh of his foreskin is not circumcised, that soul shall be cut off from his people; he hath broken my covenant. And God said unto Abraham, as for Sarai thy wife, thou shalt not call her Sarai, but Sarah shall her name be. And I will bless her and give thee a son also of her: yea, I will bless her, and she shall be a mother of nations; kings of people shall be of her. Genesis 17:10-16

God also directed Abraham to the most sacred place on the Earth and commanded him to sacrifice his only son on that very spot. This spot became the current Temple Mount in Jerusalem. Because Abraham was willing to sacrifice his only son, Isaac, then God's sacrifice of His only Son, Jesus, would qualify as fulfilling the cutting of a covenant between God and man. If Abraham had not been willing to sacrifice his only son, then God could not have sacrificed *His* only Son as part of a covenant He made with man.

Not only was Abraham in covenant with God; he also had pure human DNA all the way back to Seth and Adam. He was going to sacrifice Isaac and burn him to ashes and then stand there until God pulled his son back out of those ashes and restored him back to his father whole.

By faith Abraham, when he was tried, offered up Isaac: and he that had received the promises offered up his only begotten son, of whom it was said, that in Isaac shall thy seed be called: accounting that God was able to raise him up, even from the dead; from whence also he received him in a figure. Hebrews 11:17-19

Because Abraham had been promised that out of Isaac his seed would be called, he believed that even after he had burned his son to ashes, God, because of the covenant, would have to raise Isaac back up from the dead.

Now we begin to understand why Abraham sent Eliezer back to his family members to find a wife for Isaac. Abraham made Eliezer swear to him that he would only bring back a woman from his family lineage, for the sake of the purity of his seed. The same thing happened with Jacob. Jacob also married into the lineage of Abraham.

Now, let me digress and finish the four-hundred-year prophecy. It came to pass when Isaac and Jacob had grown up and had their own families, that Satan pushed to destroy the seed of the covenant by sending an extended famine into the land where Jacob was living. Jacob had many sons, one of them named Joseph. The story of Joseph is quite involved, but the bottom line is that God used Joseph, who was sold into slavery by his own brothers and ended up in

Egypt, to become a type of Christ. Through many very unusual circumstances, Joseph became second in command to the Pharaoh in Egypt. At the time, Egypt was a very wicked society and culture. God used Egypt to multiply the children of Israel, but He also to kept their DNA pure by segregating them in Goshen, away from the Egyptians themselves. God also placed the descendants of Abraham in a perfect position, so that when they left Egypt they would be loaded down with riches.

And he said unto Abram, Know of a surety that <u>thy</u> <u>seed</u> shall be a stranger in a land that is not theirs, and shall serve them; and they shall afflict them four hundred years; and also that nation, whom they shall serve, will I judge: and afterward shall they come out with great substance. Genesis 15:13-14

Notice in verse 13, God used the phrase *thy seed*. The battle of the ages was to keep the seed of humankind pure. Later, when Jacob, Joseph's father, moved to Egypt, Satan began to realize this. Even though the descendants of Abraham had to flee the very land God had promised them, God, in His great ability to use Satan's cleverness against him, took this opportunity to provide a way of escape for the children of Israel from the famine that would have destroyed the seed.

As it turned out, the descendants of Abraham became slaves, even as God had foretold in the prophecy given to Abraham. God, in His brilliance, knew that the children of Israel, who raised cows and sheep, would never be accepted by the Egyptians, since the Egyptians worshiped cows.

Not only were the Israelites never accepted by the Egyptians; they also grew large in number and in strength in the isolated land of Goshen. Their growth in numbers and their insistence on not assimilating with the people of Egypt eventually made them a threat to the Egyptians.

Because of the cruel slavery they experienced, the chosen people whom God was raising up were some of the most fit people on the Earth. And, because of their oppression, they were also some of the most submissive people on Earth! That sounds like God had a plan and was working out something wonderful. He was preparing the way for the coming of Jesus.

Why is this important? Because just as Jesus came the first time, He is coming back for those who love Him. Yes, you and I must learn *How to Be Rapture Ready.*

CHAPTER 8

ENTER MOSES

At the end of the four hundred years, God sent Moses to deliver Abraham's descendants from Egyptian bondage, as prophesied. Early during this four-hundred-year period of time, Satan, seeing how God had outwitted him, went to work to once again to alter the DNA in the Promised Land God had given to Abraham. We can now understand why God would later command the children of Israel to destroy every man, woman, boy and girl and all the domesticated animals in all the cities where the fallen angels had intermingled their DNA with that of mankind. This time, it appears, they had also begun to alter the DNA of the plant life and the animals within the cities they contaminated. This was the reason it took two men to carry one cluster of grapes. Giants had once again been introduced into the Earth. Is it not true today that the DNA of our seeds is being tainted by genetic modification?

As discussed earlier, God's Word says:

In the same day the LORD made a covenant with Abram, saying, Unto thy seed have I given this land, from the river of Egypt unto the great river, the river Euphrates: the Kenites, and the Kenizzites, and the Kadmonites, and the Hittites, and the Perizzites, and the Rephaims, and the Amorites, and the Canaanites, and the Girgashites, and the Jebusites.

Genesis 15:18-21

Having read the Old Testament, many people have concluded that God loved blood and warfare in the Old Testament, but He was not some genocidal monster—killing every man, woman, child and animal just because He could. The truth is that just as in the time of Noah, God had to rid the Promised Land of any altered DNA, which would destroy His plan to raise up a people who could become a Bride for His Son and who could rule and reign with Jesus. God wanted a new race of beings, one made in His image and after His likeness—body, soul and spirit—with free choice and free will.

Moses was raised up, not only under the nose of Satan, but also in the courts of a people whose DNA was clearly tainted. We do not understand many things about Egypt, but we do know that their priests moved in a powerful supernatural way, so much so that they were able to duplicate the first several miracles Moses performed among them. Egypt was a very advanced society, having greater knowledge than most of the rest of the world.

Moses was also born in a time when all Hebrew boys were supposed to be drowned in the Nile River. Satan knew of the prophecy, that at the end of four hundred years Abraham's descendants would come out of Egyptian bondage and return to the Promised Land. His plan was to destroy all the Hebrew boys born before that generation could return. Therefore, Satan moved upon Pharaoh to have all the Hebrew boys drowned in the river.

If you look at the ruling class of the Pharaohs, you will find that the elongated head covering was really a way to disguise the fact that they were "cone heads." In the recorded Egyptian history, the common people living in Egypt tied boards to their babies' heads to force their heads to be molded and shaped in an elongated way, so their children would be more accepted by the ruling class.

It appears that the genetics of ancient Egypt took the form of producing dwarfs, not gigantic beings. I believe Satan was playing with man's DNA in such a way as to produce dwarfism. Egypt even had a dwarf-god, and the Egyptians actually worshiped a god that produced dwarfs. It is strange but true that the tallest pharaoh was only about 5 feet 6 inches tall.

I believe the Egyptian people had DNA that was not pure all the way back to Adam. According to the Bible, it is very clear that Moses' DNA was pure, since he was born of Hebrew parents.

Along the way, the children of Israel encountered many situations. The following story is most fascinating, as it illustrates another time Satan orchestrated a plan to destroy the seed of the linage of Messiah to prevent Him from coming into the world.

Enter Balak and Balaam

This is the story of a heathen king named Balak and a prophet named Balaam. The children of Israel were coming to the end of their forty years of wandering through the desert when Balak hired Balaam to curse them. You may remember that, in this story, God caused a donkey to speak and correct Balaam. It was then that Balaam told Balak that he could not curse what God had blessed, but that, if Balak would send his women to intermarry with the children of Israel, within a short period of time, the children of Israel would bring the curse of God upon themselves.

It was not only the idols and the gods of the enemy that would curse the children of Israel, but more significantly, the tainting of the DNA that would curse them the most and destroy the pure DNA of their lineage.

God spoke, in the book of Revelation, that this doctrine of Baalam was really fornication:

But I have a few things against thee, because thou hast there them that hold the doctrine of Balaam, who taught Balac to cast a stumblingblock before the children of Israel, to eat things sacrificed unto idols, and to commit fornication. Revelation 2:14

Could it be that it was not the idols that concerned God the most, but the sin of having children with people who had tainted DNA? Once again, it was the tainting and intermingling of the Holy Seed. God wanted a people whose seed had not been tainted by fallen angels. This incident happened just before the children of Israel entered the Promised Land.

The Forty-Year Journey

Moses had led the children of Israel out of Egyptian bondage. Then, after forty years, they came to the Jordan River across from Jericho. However, before they could go into the Promised Land, God had some unfinished business with Moses. When the children of Israel were thirsty because of lack of water, God told Moses to strike a certain rock, and water would come forth. Moses struck the rock, and approximately three million Israelites were able to totally quench their thirst. The second time they had no water, God told Moses to speak to a certain rock and water would come forth. However, because Moses was distraught with the people, he did not speak to the rock. He beat the rock, just as he had done the first time. Because of this disobedience, God told Moses that he would not be allowed to go into Canaan (the land of promise). So, God buried Moses on the opposite side of the Jordan River from the city of Jericho.

Let me dig a little deeper into this subject with you, since this is a very special event that may be relevant to future Bible prophecy (which I will discuss later). Here is how the Bible tells the story:

And Moses went up from the plains of Moab unto the mountain of Nebo, to the top of Pisgah, that is over against Jericho. And the LORD shewed him all the land of Gilead, unto Dan, and all Naphtali, and the land of Ephraim, and Manasseh, and all the land of Judah, unto the utmost sea, and the south, and the plain of the valley of Jericho, the city of palm trees, unto Zoar. And the LORD said unto him, This is the land which I sware unto Abraham, unto Isaac, and unto Jacob, saying, I will give it unto thy seed: I have caused thee to see it with thine eyes, but thou shalt not go over thither.

So Moses the servant of the LORD died there in the land of Moab, according to the word of the LORD. And he buried him in a valley in the land of Moab, over against Beth-peor: but no man knoweth of his sepulchre unto this day. Deuteronomy 34:1-6

Notice in these verses that Moses was buried in the Valley of Moab, *"over against Jericho."* Also, take note that it would have been physically impossible for Moses to see all the land mass that God wanted to show him except by way of a supernatural experience, or vision. Could it be that God buried him in the rock that was by Himself and placed him in the same cleft where He had placed him once before?

And the LORD said, Behold, there is a place by me, and thou shalt stand upon a rock: and it shall come to pass, while my glory passeth by, that I will put thee in a clift of the rock, and will cover thee with my hand while I pass by: and I will take away mine hand, and thou shalt see my back parts: but my face shall not be seen.
Exodus 33:21-23

The most amazing thing is that the rock that was close to God and was used to hide Moses and the rock that Moses was supposed to speak to instead of beat was actually Jesus Christ Himself

BOOM!

And did all drink the same spiritual drink: for they drank of that spiritual Rock that followed them: and that Rock was Christ.   1 Corinthians 10:4

Could it be that God hid Moses in the Rock, the same cleft from which He had allowed Moses to see

79

a portion of His glory? Could God have preserved his body perfectly and could it be that this is why He would not allow Satan to know where Moses was buried? Jude 9 speaks to this truth:

> *Yet Michael the archangel, when contending with the devil he disputed about the body of Moses, durst not bring against him a railing accusation, but said, The Lord rebuke thee.*

I will elaborate more on this point later in the book. As we progress, keep in mind the subject and purpose of the book, *How to Be Rapture Ready.*

CHAPTER 9

ENTER RUTH

The next item to consider is the following question: What about the purity of the lineage of Christ since Ruth, His ancestor, was thought to be coming from the land of Moab and was called "a Moabitess"?

Most pastors who have not researched this subject are not aware of the facts that define the lineage of the daughter-in-law of Naomi. Upon researching this subject, it is clear that Ruth, in fact, was an Israelite and a descendant of Abraham all the way back to Adam!

Remember, God chose David to be king over Israel, and David was a direct descendant of Ruth and Boaz. God sent the prophet Samuel to anoint David to become king. He was not looking for someone who was talented, handsome, tall in stature or well educated. He wanted a specific man He Himself had chosen.

According to the Scriptures, we know that David was not tall like Saul. There is no talk of him being talented, educated or anything else that would have made him stand out, that he should be chosen to be king. Nothing, that is, until Samuel laid hands on him, anointed him with oil and prophesied over him. With this in mind, remember the following verses:

And Nahshon begat Salma, and Salma begat Boaz, and Boaz begat Obed, and Obed begat Jesse.
1 Chronicles 2:11-12

An Ammonite or Moabite shall not enter into the congregation of the LORD; even to their tenth generation shall they not enter into the congregation of the LORD for ever.
Deuteronomy 23:3

Let me emphasize: The descendants of Moab were not allowed to entre the holy Temple! If anyone married a descendant of Moab, their descendants were not allowed to enter the Temple for ten generations. The Jewish people could trace their lineage all the way back to Adam, and they would have been fully aware of David's lineage. If David's great-grandmother had been a Moabite, he would not have been allowed to enter the Temple, and David's son, Solomon, the next king to follow him, would also not have been allowed to enter the Temple.

What does it all mean? Ruth, David's great-grandmother, may well have been from the land of Moab, but she could not have been of the lineage of Moab.

If she had been, her DNA would have been tainted by the intermarriage of the fallen angels with women. God would have known this, and the people would have known it too. God would not have allowed that tainted DNA into Jesus' bloodline, and the Jewish people would not have allowed David to be their king or to enter their Temple.

I am convinced that Ruth's bloodline was untainted all the way back to Adam. Therefore, Jesus can be seated on the throne of David, who was a descendant of Ruth. There can be no question of the purity of Ruth's bloodline.

Is it all relevant? It is, and we will see how. In the meantime, keep your focus on the need to get ready for what is to come. We must all know *How to Be Rapture Ready*.

CHAPTER 10

ENTER ZEPHANIAH

I am going to allow myself to be sidetracked here so that tI can begin the story of the dealings of God in reference to the coming of the Seed of the woman. Jeremiah was born in 640 BC, so he was a contemporary of Zephaniah (who wrote his book in 624 BC). We do not know the exact year Zephaniah was born, but he was definitely a prophet in the same time period as Jeremiah.

Zephaniah also shared a prophetic word about a time that would come when Messiah, the Seed of the woman, is manifested. At that time, the language of Heaven will be restored to the Earth:

Therefore wait ye upon me, saith the LORD, until the day that I rise up to the prey: for my determination is to gather the nations, that I may assemble the kingdoms, to pour upon them mine indignation, even all my fierce anger: for all the earth shall be devoured with the fire of my jealousy. For then will I turn to the people a pure language, that they may all call upon the name of the LORD, to serve him with one consent.

Zephaniah 3:8-9

BOOM!

What could this be referring to except the language of Heaven? In 1 Corinthians 13:1, Paul wrote this:

Though I speak with the tongues of men or of angels … .

In God's perspective, there are only two languages: the tongues of men and the tongues of angels. We know that God taught Adam and Eve how to talk. Could it be that they learned the language of Heaven? God confounded the language of men at the tower of Babel. The Scriptures tell the story in Genesis 11:1:

And the whole world was of one language and of one speech.

This was in the context of the building of the tower of Babel.

And the LORD came down to see the city and the tower, which the children of men builded. And the LORD said, Behold, the people is one, and they have all one language; and this they begin to do: and now nothing will be restrained from them, which they have imagined to do. Go to, let us go down, and there confound their language, that they may not understand one another's speech.   Genesis 11:5-7

I believe that the language the whole world spoke and understood at that time was the tongue of angels Paul spoke of in First Corinthians. It is the language of Heaven and has no confusion in it. Every language of the world, every tongue of mankind, has confusion built into it. For example, in English when we say the word *read,* people do not know what we are saying because the word *read* sounds exactly like the word *reed,* but the meaning of the two words is totally different. We cannot distinguish what a person is referring to except by understanding the context.

In the same way, if we say *red,* this word sounds just like another use of the word *read,* as in the sentence "I read a book yesterday." Scientists have declared that the biggest problem with languages today is from the confusion built into the words. When people discuss problems in their work, inevitably the biggest problem they have is with communication. Understanding each other is not always easy.

I believe that, in Genesis 11, when God took the ability of man to speak and understand the language of Heaven, men were no longer able to focus on their projects as they could before. God was concerned with their method of communication, not the height of their tower.

In Daniel 5 Belshazzar, the king of Babylon, held a feast, and a very strange thing happened. At one point, a hand appeared, writing on the wall. Belshazzar demanded an interpretation of the writing, calling for all the wise men of Babylon to translate it. But no one could be found who understood what the writing was saying. That is ... until Daniel was called. This would indicate that the writing was not in any known language of the world.

Daniel did not actually translate the writing either. He referred to what he understood it to say as an *"interpretation,"* not a translation. This is what he said the written message meant:

And this is the writing that was written, MENE, MENE, TEKEL, UPHARSIN. This is the interpretation of the thing: MENE; God hath numbered thy kingdom, and finished it. TEKEL; Thou art weighed in the balances, and art found wanting. PERES; Thy kingdom is divided, and given to the Medes and Persians.

Daniel 5:25-28

BOOM!

There is a very big difference between translation and interpretation.

The prophet Isaiah foretold a coming day:

For with stammering lips and another tongue will he speak to this people. To whom he said, This is the rest wherewith ye may cause the weary to rest; and this is the refreshing: yet they would not hear.

Isaiah 28:11-12

He said that the people who would refuse this miracle would *"fall backward, and be broken, and snared, and taken"* (Isaiah 28:13). Could it be that Zephaniah saw God giving back to man a portion of what He had withdrawn at the tower of Babel?

Now compare Zephaniah 3:8-9 with what is written in Acts 1 and 2:

Zephaniah 3:8 *Wait ye upon me, saith the* LORD
Acts 1:4 *Wait for the promise of the Father*

Zephaniah 3:8 *My determination is to gather the nations*
Acts 2:5 *There were dwelling at Jerusalem Jews, devout men, out of every nation under heaven*

Zephaniah 3:9 *I will turn to the people a pure language*
Acts 2:4 *And they were all filled with the Holy Ghost and began to speak with other tongues as the Spirit gave them utterance*

Zephaniah 3:9 *To serve him with one consent*
Acts 2:1 *They were all with one accord in one place*

I have addressed this because it is an example of what God desires for humanity. One day, the Word of God shows, we will judge angels (see 1 Corinthians 6:3). When we see Jesus as He is, we will become the manifested sons of God. That is Rapture time. I will address this more later in the book. Please keep reading!

Many preach that we are already the manifested sons of God, but I fear that they are deceived. When we see Jesus, the ninety-three percent of our brain and spirit that we have only slightly used until now will suddenly be turned on. We have all the wherewithal to operate in the supernatural, but because of the fall of man, we must yield to the Holy Spirit to tap into that realm on a limited basis. When we yield to the Holy Spirit, we speak mysteries to God in tongues, but we do not understand what we are saying ... unless we move into the gift of interpretation of tongues. When we get to Heaven, we will speak and understand the language of Heaven just as naturally as we speak and understand our native earthly language today.

To explain our limited use of brain capacity, I want to refer to some unusual people. We call a person exhibiting singularly brilliant abilities in one particular area an *idiot savant*. Scientists cannot explain how a person who has never had music lessons can perfectly play Bach or Beethoven. Neither can they explain individuals who can look at a page full of numbers and, without any apparent calculation, almost instantly announce the total of the numbers on the page. It is as if part of their mind is unlocked in an area of brilliance that is inaccessible to the rest of us. It is my opinion that these rare abilities are dormant in us.

Other examples include those who have come upon the scene of an accident and are somehow able to lift a car or truck weighing tons in order to free a trapped person. When we are changed, *"in a moment, in the twinkling of an eye,"* we will move naturally in what people today call the supernatural. The baptism of the Holy Spirit is the springboard into the supernatural realm of God. The operation of the gifts of the Holy Spirit is as if (in a very limited way) our natural minds and the Holy Spirit within us are in sync, to impart to us the supernatural.

Zephaniah prophesied about what would happen several hundred years later. Why would any human reject what was spoken by the prophets Isaiah, Zephaniah and Joel? In New Testament times, John wrote:

Beloved, now are we the sons of God, and it doth not yet appear what we shall be: but we know that, when he shall appear, we shall be like him; for we shall see him as he is.   1 John 3:2

When Jesus returns in the Rapture, we shall be changed, and we will be able to do what Christ did after His resurrection. We will be able to disappear, walk through walls, walk on water and be translated, so that we can rule and reign with Him. We will also be able to speak the tongue of angels and understand perfectly what we are saying. Hallelujah! If that sounds good to you, then you need to learn *How to Be Rapture Ready*.

ENTER DANIEL

It seems that over the centuries Israel always progressed from repentance to complacency, from obedience to disobedience, from favor to disfavor with God. So, in the days of Jeremiah, God told the prophet that His people would go into bondage for seventy years. During this terrible time, once again, God raised up special leaders (such as Daniel and his three Hebrew friends) the same way He raised up Joseph and Moses, to be a godly influence and bring deliverance to the special linage of the holy seed. Daniel and his three Hebrew friends were ordained by God to watch over this seventy year oppression.

In Daniel 9, as Daniel was fasting, clothed in sackcloth and sitting on ashes, the angel Gabriel appeared to him and gave him the most phenomenal Messianic prophecy in the whole of the Bible. This prophecy foretold the very year the Messiah would be *"cut off."* Gabriel said that this would begin when the command was given to rebuild Jerusalem. This prophecy would not begin to be fulfilled until many years later. God even used two different heathen potentates to set things in motion for the fulfillment of the prophecy.

I don't have space here to fully expound on this prophecy. However, I will say that the word of the Lord spoken to Daniel about the seventieth (or last) week is about to begin soon. The seventieth week is what Bible scholars call "The Great Tribulation." I will try to summarize the prophecy without going into too much detail:

Daniel 9:24

Seventy weeks are determined upon thy people and upon thy holy city [Jerusalem],
To finish the transgression, ...
To make an end of sins,
To make reconciliation for iniquity,
To bring in everlasting righteousness,
To seal up the vision and prophecy, ...
To anoint the most Holy.

The schedule of events—70 weeks total: 7 weeks + 62 weeks + 1 final week—every prophetic week being a period of seven years.

From the going forth of the commandment to restore and to build [or rebuild] *Jerusalem unto the Messiah the Prince shall be seven weeks, and threescore and two weeks* (which is a total of sixty-nine weeks of years, or 483 years) (see verse 25). In *seven weeks* (or 49 years) *the street shall be built again and the wall, even in troublesome times* (same verse).

In an additional sixty-two weeks of years after the streets and walls are rebuilt, Messiah shall be cut off. It was the year that Jesus was crucified.

But not for himself ...

For the people (verse 26).

Jesus was crucified precisely at the end of the sixty-ninth week, just as the angel had told Daniel it would happen.

Verses 26 and 27 speak of desolations. *"The people that will come will destroy the city and the sanctuary."* The city of Jerusalem was destroyed in 70 AD, and the Sanctuary was destroyed along with it. Yet to come is the seventieth week of years, the final week of the Daniel 9 prophecy.

"And he shall confirm the covenant with many for one week." Antichrist is to confirm a covenant with many in Israel.

"In the midst of the week he shall cause the sacrifice and the oblation to cease." Halfway through this week (three and a half years), the Antichrist will cause the sacrifice and the evening oblation to cease.

Most teachers of Bible prophecy believe that half-way through the Tribulation the Antichrist will go into the Temple and precipitate an event that is described as *"the abomination that maketh desolate"* (Daniel 11:31). This is alluded to in Daniel 9:27 (*"the overspreading of abominations"*) and also in Daniel 12:11. Jesus also spoke of this in Matthew 24:15 and Mark 13:14.

It is amazing when you realize that, according to the Jewish calendar, the time from the command given to Nehemiah to rebuild Jerusalem until Messiah was crucified was exactly 483 years. It is commonly accepted that in the book of Daniel one week represents seven years. **Seven weeks plus 62 weeks = 69 prophetic weeks, and** 69 prophetic weeks times 7 years makes a total of 483 years.

Coming to the right figure here is complicated by the fact that the Gregorian Calendar has 365 days to the year, and the Jewish calendar only has 360 days per year, with an additional month added every few years to make up the difference.

I'm also very aware that this calculation is not perfectly explained or justified here. My illustration is simply presented to make a point about the sequence of prophetic events. God does not tell us exact dates when a prophetic event will begin, but He also never leaves us without hope.

You can see, in Daniel 12:25, that the angel of the Lord never prophesied the year that Messiah would be born, but He prophesied the year that redemption would be completed. Isn't that wonderful! I see here the grace of God being manifested. No man (nor even

Satan) would know the year the Messiah would be born, but the Jews would have been able to calculate the exact year Messiah would be cut off because of this prophecy. Perhaps that's why Anna and Simeon were looking for the coming of the Messiah around the time of Jesus' actual birth (see Luke 2).

No one knew the year that Christ was to be born, but the year He was to be "cut off" had been prophesied hundreds of years before His crucifixion. Even Caiaphas, the high priest at the time, alluded to this during a discussion about the miracles Jesus did:

> *And one of them, named Caiaphas, being the high priest that same year, said unto them, Ye know nothing at all, nor consider that it is expedient for us, that one man should die for the people, and that the whole nation perish not.*
> *And this spake he not of himself: but being high priest that year, he prophesied that Jesus should die for that nation; and not for that nation only, but that also he should gather together in one the children of God that were scattered abroad. Then from that day forth they took counsel together for to put him to death.*
>
> John 11:49-53

BOOM!

True, Caiaphas was the high priest, but he was more concerned with the political ramifications than he was with the coming of the Messiah. He might not even have understood that this prophecy in Daniel was referring to the Messiah. Most importantly, he did not want his position, that of High Priest, to be threatened by the Roman government.

Wow! **Sixty-nine weeks have been fulfilled,** and now **we are waiting for the seventieth week of Daniel to begin**. How I would like to write in detail about this matter, but I must stay focused on the subject at hand. Bible scholars all over the world agree that the seventieth week of Daniel will signal the beginning of the Great Tribulation.

Even Jesus, in Luke 4:16-20, after finding a particular place of prophecy in Isaiah 61:1-2, stopped before completing the reading of verse 2, leaving out the part that says, *"the day of the vengeance of our God."* He quoted Isaiah:

The Spirit of the LORD God is upon me; because the LORD hath anointed me to preach good tidings unto the meek; he hath sent me to bind up the brokenhearted, to proclaim liberty to the captives, and the opening of the prison to them that are bound; to proclaim the acceptable year of the LORD.

After Jesus read this passage from Isaiah, He then closed the book, gave it to the rabbi and sat down, declaring, *"This day is this scripture fulfilled in your ears"* (Luke 4:21). **He purposely left out the reference to the**

seventieth week—*"the day of the vengeance of our God."*

When Jesus was crucified, the sixty-ninth prophetic week was finished. **The seventieth week of Daniel would remain on hold for two thousand years, possibly even until our day**.

Daniel read in the prophecy of Jeremiah that the Israelites would be in captivity for seventy years. By that time, he would have been a very old man, possibly in his eighties. He had been a youth when he was taken into captivity. He was a contemporary of Nehemiah, Ezra, Esther, Zechariah and Zephaniah.

The following scripture passage contains the story Daniel told of the angel of the Lord speaking about the seventy weeks of prophecy recorded in Chapter 9 of the book that bears his name. I will go into greater detail about this prophecy later in the book. For now, I want to quote the entire prophecy here so that you can read it in its entirety.

> *And whiles I was speaking, and praying, and confessing my sin and the sin of my people Israel, and presenting my supplication before the LORD my God for the holy mountain of my God; yea, whiles I was speaking in prayer, even the man Gabriel, whom I had seen in the vision at the beginning, being caused to fly swiftly, touched me about the time of the evening oblation. And he informed me, and talked with me, and said, O Daniel, I am now come forth to give thee skill and*

understanding. At the beginning of thy supplications the commandment came forth, and I am come to shew thee; for thou art greatly beloved: therefore understand the matter, and consider the vision.

Seventy weeks are determined upon thy people and upon thy holy city, to finish the transgression, and to make an end of sins, and to make reconciliation for iniquity, and to bring in everlasting righteousness, and to seal up the vision and prophecy, and to anoint the most Holy.

Know therefore and understand, that from the going forth of the commandment to restore and to build Jerusalem unto the Messiah the Prince shall be seven weeks, and threescore and two weeks: the street shall be built again, and the wall, even in troublous times. And after threescore and two weeks shall Messiah be cut off, but not for himself: and the people of the prince that shall come shall destroy the city and the sanctuary; and the end thereof shall be with a flood, and unto the end of the war desolations are determined. And he shall confirm the covenant with many for one week: and in the midst of the week he shall cause the sacrifice and the oblation to cease, and for the overspreading of abominations he shall make it desolate, even until the consummation, and that determined shall be poured upon the desolate. Daniel 9:20-27

Many Bible scholars believe that in Daniel 12, the angel prophesied the end of the Tribulation. We do not know when the Tribulation will begin; however, the angel said that from the time of the abomination of desolation being set up in the Temple to the end of the tribulation would be exactly 1,290 days, or three and a half years. Once again, in perilous times, God gives us the day that those times will end. He never leaves us without hope.

Now, we will discuss Daniel's contemporaries, and as we do, remember the focus of this book and let God show you by His Spirit *How to Be Rapture Ready.*

CHAPTER 12

ENTER THREE OTHER HISTORICAL FIGURES

Enter Nehemiah

It was not those in high religious positions whom God chose to start these events and bring the Jewish lineage out of captivity. Instead, God used a heathen king, Artaxerxes, to begin the prophetic time clock of Daniel's seventy weeks. Then God gave a simple Jewish cupbearer favor with the ruler of Babylon. It was not a prophet, a priest, or a Jewish leader, but Nehemiah, the king's cupbearer, who was given the permission, resources, and a command to rebuild the walls of Jerusalem. Nehemiah also carried a letter written by the king to the neighboring governors telling them to allow him to do this work and to supply him the needed materials.

It was around 450 BC that Nehemiah obtained permission to go back to Jerusalem and rebuild the city. It was that precise moment when God's prophetic time clock began ticking for the countdown for the Seed of the woman to be born and the redemption of human-kind to be completed.

In the process of time, when Nehemiah began to share his mission with the governors beyond the river, the word of this mission leaked out to those who were assigned by Satan to hold the city of Jerusalem in ruins. Two men, Sanballat and Tobiah, immediately began to make trouble for Nehemiah. When Nehemiah shared his mission with the Jewish leaders, notice the following:

> *Then said I unto them, Ye see the distress that we are in, how Jerusalem lieth waste, and the gates thereof are burned with fire: come, and let us build up the wall of Jerusalem, that we be no more a reproach. Then I told them of the hand of my God which was good upon me; as also the king's words that he had spoken unto me.*
>
> *And they said, Let us rise up and build. So they strengthened their hands for this good work.*
>
> *But when Sanballat the Horonite, and Tobiah the servant, the Ammonite, and Geshem the Arabian, heard it, they laughed us to scorn, and despised us, and said, What is this thing that ye do? Will ye rebel against the king?*
>
> *Then answered I them, and said unto them, The God of heaven, he will prosper us; therefore we his servants will arise and build: but ye have no portion, nor right, nor memorial, in Jerusalem.*   Nehemiah 2:17-20

Notice also who these men were. They were: Sanballat, an Horonite, Tobiah, an Ammonite, and Geshem, an Arabian. I don't know who the Arabian was. but the other two were part of a tainted DNA people controlled by Satan to hinder a very prophetic event that was necessary to bring the Messiah, who was of totally pure DNA all the way back to Adam.

Enter Ezra

During this same period, Ezra was brought forward by God to challenge the Jewish seed to revival. Furthermore, we will now see why God demanded that all the men of Israel had to get rid of their heathen wives. God specifically named the Egyptian women. Also notice the "ites" that are listed in Ezra 9:1-2 below.

King Darius had told Ezra to go back to Jerusalem and rebuild the Jewish temple. Ezra rebuilt the altar, but he failed to rebuild the rest of the temple because of resistance from the local inhabitants. The local people were happy to be living with the *status quo.* However, when Ezra returned to Jerusalem, he was able to address a major problem concerning Jewish society. Tainted DNA, due to the willful ways of the Jewish people, had to be dwelt with. Ezra wrote:

Now when these things were done, the princes came to me, saying, The people of Israel, and the priests, and the Levites, have not separated themselves from the people *of the lands, doing according to their abominations, even of the <u>Canaanites, the Hittites, the Perizzites, the Jebusites, the Ammonites, the Moabites, the Egyptians, and the Amorites</u>. For they have taken of their daughters for themselves, and for their sons: <u>so that the holy seed have mingled themselves</u> with the people of those lands: yea, the hand of the princes and rulers hath been chief in this trespass.*   Ezra 9:1-2

BOOM!

Notice verse 2 states that they had mingled their seed with the people of those lands. The men of that time agreed with the elders, and they sat down over a period of many weeks to decide how to resolve this issue. Most Bible scholars agree that they then met with their foreign wives to divorce them and make settlements with them, so that the women could be sent away. Thus, the matter was concluded, and God and His people worked through this most difficult situation.

It is necessary to reemphasize that the real issue was the mixing of their seed with foreign women, thus potentially introducing tainted DNA into the lineage of Christ.

Enter Esther: The Salvation of the Holy Seed

Needless to say, the story of Esther is another of the stories showing how God protected the seed of the Jewish people for the coming of the Messiah. The story of the Israelites, throughout history, is the story of God preserving the Jewish seed that Satan has constantly tried to destroy. Even after the Messiah came, the Jewish nation was important to God. His concern was not just preserving the Jewish people, but also preserving the integrity of the Abrahamic Covenant and the Word of God.

Throughout history, Satan has continued to try to make the Word of God fail. He has made a heroic effort to destroy the Jewish people, to prevent Genesis 3:15 from being fulfilled. As we have seen, this is the battle of the ages, and the goal has been (and continues to be) the destruction of the pure DNA of humankind. One reason I believe there is a God is that there are still Jews alive in our world, and many of them. God has miraculously preserved them.

The next character in the drama of the centuries is Zechariah. As we study him and his part in the drama, keep in mind what our focus is: *How to Be Rapture Ready.*

CHAPTER 13

ENTER ZECHARIAH
AN UNUSUAL VISION OF THE LAST DAYS

Sometime before the fourth year of King Darius' reign, the angel of the Lord appeared to Zechariah, and they had the following exchange of words:

Then I turned, and lifted up mine eyes, and looked, and behold a flying roll.

And he said unto me, What seest thou? And I answered, I see a flying roll; the length thereof is twenty cubits, and the breadth thereof ten cubits.

Then said he unto me, This is the curse that goes forth over the face of the whole earth: for every one that steals shall be cut off as on this side according to it; and every one that swears shall be cut off as on that side according to it. I will bring it forth, saith the LORD of hosts, and it shall enter into the house of the thief, and into the house of him that swears falsely by my name: and it shall remain in the midst of his

*house, and shall consume it with the timber thereof
and the stones thereof.* Zechariah 5:1-4

One night I was caught up in the Spirit and saw this scripture come to life. I only mention this because it has to do with the Mark of the Beast and the DNA of mankind. My brother Mike had asked me a very interesting question one afternoon. As I was musing over his question, I saw Zechariah 5 come into focus and understood how this could refer to the Mark of the Beast.

Mike had asked me if there were two unpardonable sins, and I had answered him that there is only one unpardonable sin—blasphemy against the Holy Spirit! He then asked, "Why is it, then, that if a person takes the Mark in his right hand or forehead, he cannot simply cut it out of his skin or dig it out of his skin and repent? Why is it that the book of Revelation says that once the Mark is received by a person, they are doomed forever?"

The passage he referred to is in Revelation 14:

*And the third angel followed them, saying with
a loud voice, If any man worship the beast and
his image, and receive his mark in his forehead,
or in his hand, the same shall drink of the wine
of the wrath of God, which is poured out without*

mixture into the cup of his indignation; and he shall be tormented with fire and brimstone in the presence of the holy angels, and in the presence of the Lamb: and the smoke of their torment ascendeth up forever and ever: and they have no rest day nor night, who worship the beast and his image, and whosoever receiveth the mark of his name.

Revelation 14:9-11

That line of reasoning from my brother got me thinking: *Why couldn't a person remove the Mark of the Beast and repent? Could it be that something happens to a person when they willingly take the Mark?* That is when the Holy Spirit whispered in my ear and caused me to remember the angel of the Lord's dealing with Zechariah in a very unusual exchange. Here is what the Spirit of God began showing me:

In Zechariah 5:2, the angel of the Lord asked Zechariah what he saw. Zechariah answered, *"I see a flying roll; the length thereof is twenty cubits, and the breadth thereof ten cubits."* The "roll" that Zechariah saw was a scroll. It was fifteen feet wide and thirty feet tall, and it looked like it had wings. This is very close in size to the many low-orbit satellites that are going around the Earth today in space (see the picture on the next page).

111

There are many different shapes of satellites. Some look just like a scroll when they have their solar panels extended. It is these solar panels that make all satellites appear to have wings.

Several decades ago, Motorola put up around three hundred satellites around Earth in low orbit, so that they could cover all the inhabited areas of the planet. These satellites were at an elevation of between three and five hundred miles above the surface of the Earth.

Originally, satellites had been placed in orbit at more than 22,000 miles above Earth's surface so they could stay in one area and still synchronize with the spin of the Earth on its axis. They had to be at that altitude to be able to stay fixed in outer space and not go off into deep space or fall back to Earth. It was the perfect position so that the gravitational pull of the Earth would keep them in perfect orbit.

The problem with this arrangement was that it took too long for a signal to go that distance and return to Earth. It also required the use of a very large dish to receive the signal from that deep in space. Consequently scientists came up with the idea of locating satellites much closer to Earth. In this way, they could accommodate tasks such as GPS use with much smaller dishes. This new plan included making the satellites go into a lower Earth orbit at a much higher rate of speed and passing off communications signals smoothly to the next available satellite. This kept information from being lost.

In the following drawing, see the alignment of satellites in low Earth orbit (LEO).

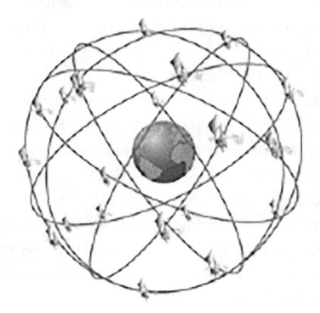

The angel of the Lord said to Zechariah:

Then said he unto me, This is the curse that goeth forth over the face of the whole earth: for every one that stealeth shall be cut off as on this side according to it; and every one that sweareth shall be cut off as on that side according to it.   Zechariah 5:3

God showed me that the current satellite system would one day be capable, not only of tracking a person, but also recording every place that person had gone over a period of many days. Also, the person's voice will be recorded and the recordings stored for extended periods of time on a chip or whatever instrument is used in the makeup of the Mark of the Beast. All the authorities will have to do is to scan the Mark to verify a person's location at any given time, for example, during a robbery.

Also, satellites will record to your Mark every word spoken for at least the past three to six months, so that whatever is spoken at any crime scene can be used as evidence against you.

This brings me back to the subject at hand — the DNA of mankind and Satan's obsession with destroying it. The book of Revelation is clear that every person who takes the Mark of the Beast will be assigned to Hell forever!

CONTENTS

And the third angel followed them, saying with a loud voice, If any man worship the beast and his image, and receive his mark in his forehead, or in his hand, the same shall drink of the wine of the wrath of God, which is poured out without mixture into the cup of his indignation; and he shall be tormented with fire and brimstone in the presence of the holy angels, and in the presence of the Lamb: and the smoke of their torment ascends up forever and ever: and they have no rest day nor night, who worship the beast and his image, and whosoever receives the mark of his name.

Revelation 14:9-11

And I saw the beast, and the kings of the earth, and their armies, gathered together to make war against him that sat on the horse, and against his army. And the beast was taken, and with him the false prophet that wrought miracles before him, with which he deceived them that had received the mark of the beast, and them that worshipped his image. These both were cast alive into a lake of fire burning with brimstone.

Revelation 19:19-20

Along this line of reasoning, I believe that everyone who takes the Mark of the Beast will have their DNA changed in their body so that they will no longer be entirely human. **BOOM!**

Otherwise, why couldn't they simply remove the instrument of the Mark and repent? Consider these key words spoken by Jesus:

And as it was in the days of Noe, so shall it be also in the days of the Son of man. They did eat, they drank, they married wives, they were given in marriage, until the day that Noah entered into the ark ... .

Luke 17:26-27

Who was marrying in the days of Noah? The fallen angels were intermarrying with the human race to destroy the DNA of humankind, in an effort to keep the Seed of the woman from bruising Satan's head. Jesus was saying, "When the Son of man returns, there will be another attempt to try to destroy the seed of mankind."

The Mark of the Beast will make everyone who receives it become mean-spirited. People will become desperate to destroy the plan of God in the Earth, just as the giants in the book of Genesis. Since taking the mark will prevent them from having access to Heaven, they will have nothing to lose!

Remember what God said:

And God saw that the wickedness of man was great in the earth, and that every imagination of the thoughts of his heart was only evil continually.

Genesis 6:5

If their DNA is changed, they will be like the Nephilim (giants) who were semi-spirit beings and were described as those whose thinking was *"only evil continually."* **BOOM!**

To summarize, the Mark of the Beast will have to communicate with the curse that goes over the face of the whole Earth so that every person who has the Mark can be tracked, their voice recorded, and the DNA of each person changed, so that they are no longer one hundred percent human.

I believe that this DNA change will be presented to all humanity as a means to extend their life by twenty-five to fifty years. This change, it will be said, would make it easy for doctors to cure illnesses through a person's DNA. Already, doctors are taking DNA from a person's heart, repairing it and then putting it back in the damaged organ to fix the damage. There is not a week that goes by that we do not hear in the news about someone tampering with our DNA.

Not so long ago I read that scientists were hoping to introduce a vaccine for the Covid-19 virus that would grow in our bodies attached to a bone close to the place where the vaccine was introduced. **BOOM!** This would make it permanently effective and prevent us from getting the virus ever again. I do not know if this is true, but, if something like this is possible, it would be easy to see how our DNA could be adversely affected. **BOOM!**

What does it all mean? It means that the coming of Jesus is nearer than ever before and that you and I need to learn *How to Be Rapture Ready.*

CHAPTER 14

ENTER MALACHI
THE PRONOUNCEMENT OF THE CURSE

Chronologically, the prophecy of Malachi comes immediately after the prophecies of Zechariah and Nehemiah. Zechariah wrote from 520 to 518 BC. Nehemiah wrote his book in 415 BC and died in 405 BC. Malachi was born in 424 BC and wrote his book around 397 BC.

In Malachi 4:5-6, the prophet made one of the most profound prophecies ever written. He said that *"before the coming of the great and dreadful day of the Lord,"* God would send Elijah the prophet and turn the hearts of the fathers to the children and the hearts of the children to their fathers *"lest [He] come and smite the earth with a curse."* For this reason, during the Passover Seder, the Jews set an extra place at the table for Elijah. They believe that when he comes, Messiah will be sure to follow.

Jesus was asked about this prophecy:

And they asked him, saying, Why say the scribes that Elias must first come? And he answered and told them, Elias verily cometh first, and restoreth all things; and how it is written of the Son of man, that he must suffer many things, and be set at nought. But I say unto you, That Elias is indeed come, and they have done unto him whatsoever they listed, as it is written of him.

Mark 9:11-13

Jesus also declared:

And from the days of John the Baptist until now the kingdom of heaven suffereth violence, and the violent take it by force. For all the prophets and the law prophesied until John. And if ye will receive it, this is Elias, which was for to come. He that hath ears to hear, let him hear. Matthew 11:12-15

Notice again the last two verses in the Old Testament:

Behold, I will send you Elijah the prophet before the coming of the great and dreadful day of the LORD: and he shall turn the heart of the fathers to the children, and the heart of the children to their fathers, lest I come and smite the earth with a curse.

Malachi 4:5-6

We have been taught all our lives that we are under the Age of Grace, but God calls this period of time after the rejection of Christ a curse. Elijah came, and the High Priest knew it all too well. But, still, the people Jesus came to first, His own people, rejected this gracious and loving gift from their Father, God.

Once again, I refer you to what I quoted earlier in the book:

And one of them, named Caiaphas, being the high priest that same year, said unto them, Ye know nothing at all, nor consider that it is expedient for us, that one man should die for the people, and that the whole nation perish not. And this spake he not of himself: but being high priest that year, he prophesied that Jesus should die for that nation.   John 11:49-51

Daniel's prophecy was clear as to the exact year the Messiah would be cut off. Only the elite priests were allowed to study the book of Daniel. Caiaphas was aware of the prophecy of Daniel 9. He was referring to it when he made this statement. The dye was cast, and the rejection of Jesus was complete.

In Matthew 27:24-25, when Pilate washed his hands to signify that he was innocent of Jesus being crucified, the Jews shouted: *"His blood be on us, and on our children"* (verse 25). At that time, the world truly opened the door for the Dark Ages that began approximately four hundred years later. The Renaissance did not begin until the fifteenth or sixteenth century. But, according to Malachi 4:6, we have been under a curse, not grace, for the past two thousand years.

If, on the Day of Pentecost, the leaders of the Jews had accepted the preaching of Peter proclaiming Jesus as the Messiah and repented, then God could have shortened the time, and the Tribulation could have begun. If that had happened, within seven years, mankind could have been in the Millennium. We will never know if that could have been. However, we *do* know that these two thousand plus years were hidden from Satan because Paul wrote:

But we speak the wisdom of God in a mystery, even the hidden wisdom, which God ordained before the world unto our glory: which none of the princes of this world knew: for had they known it, they would not have crucified the Lord of glory.   1 Corinthians 2:7-8

BOOM!

Here Paul makes it clear that God hid this mystery from Satan, for he wrote, *"had the princes of this world known, they would not have crucified the Lord of glory!"* Regardless, the world went through a extremely dark period wherein the Word of God was almost destroyed from off the face of the Earth. It was hidden from the common man. Religious services were spoken in Latin, which only the priests could understand.

In spite of the strategy of Satan, God preserved His Word, using the very system Satan was using to try to wipe it out. Thus the Word of God was saved. Yes, God used the Catholic Church to preserve His Word in the same way that He had groomed the deliverer of Israel, Moses, right under Pharaoh's nose.

Let me take a moment and prove to you that we have been in the Age of the Curse. Man did not advance in any significant way during the Dark Ages. When you consider his mode of transportation, it remained the same for two thousand years. However, in just the past hundred and twenty-five years, we have made advances beyond mankind's wildest dreams. We drive, we fly, and we talk over long distances on cellphones. We have electricity, and we broadcast invisible pictures through the air all over the world. These pictures are received through antennas and are seen by people on their cellphones and TV sets. So many modern advances have been made that if you brought back George Washington today, he would think we were all operating in the supernatural! **BOOM!**

Around the end of the nineteenth century, I believe, we began to see the curse lift. The prophet Joel prophesied: *"in the last days, saith God, I will pour out of my Spirit upon all flesh..."*. The Azusa Street Revival, led by a humble black man whose last name was William J. Seymour, began to "see more" than many of his peers by the power of the Holy Spirit. He received the baptism in the Holy

Spirit, and, with stammering lips and another tongue, the Holy Spirit began speaking through man again.

The revival began as a true interracial movement, with white people praying for black people and black people praying for white people. For whatever reasons, two separate large churches, the Church of God in Christ and the Assemblies of God, were formed at this time. Aside from the racial connotations, it was a sign of great things to come. God was moving once again among His people. **BOOM!**

A word of encouragement needs to be placed here to cheer up the reader. Even though this age was pronounced by God through Malachi as being a curse, it was all in His plan. God hid this age from Satan, not sharing this period of two thousand years with any of His prophets—because He needed this time to develop a Bride for His Son.

When the Bible says that a third of the stars fell from Heaven, most Bible scholars interpret that as a third of the angels falling from Heaven, but Jesus said:

I beheld Satan as lightning fall from heaven.

Luke 10:18

Most Bible scholars believe that Satan was formerly an archangel and, probably, the worship director of Heaven. Regardless, there is no reference in the Bible that God ever replaced those fallen angels. I cannot

124

preach what I am about to say as fact, but allow me to share a concept that might explain why God did not replace the fallen angels. Is it possible that what John the Baptist said, while walking on the Earth, with regard to the Old Testament saints and all that came after the resurrection of Christ, might shed light on all of this? Here's what he said:

John answered and said, A man can receive nothing, except it be given him from heaven. Ye yourselves bear me witness, that I said, I am not the Christ, but that I am sent before him. He that hath the bride is the bridegroom: but the friend of the bridegroom, which standeth and heareth him, rejoiceth greatly because of the bridegroom's voice: this my joy therefore is fulfilled. He must increase, but I must decrease. John 3: 27-30

What John was saying is that he was a friend of the Bridegroom. Revelation 20:6 declares:

Blessed and holy is he that hath part in the first resurrection: on such the second death hath no power, but they shall be priests of God and of Christ, and shall reign with him a thousand years. Revelation 20:6

Here John the Revelator was saying that all who are a part of the first resurrection will rule with Christ for a thousand years.

Here is more scriptural confirmation:

The Spirit itself beareth witness with our spirit, that we are the children of God: and if children, then heirs; heirs of God, and joint-heirs with Christ; if so be that we suffer with him, that we may be also glorified together. For I reckon that the sufferings of this present time are not worthy to be compared with the glory which shall be revealed in us. For the earnest expectation of the creature waiteth for the manifestation of the sons of God.   Romans 8:16-19

If we are children of God, then we are heirs of God and joint-heirs with Christ. We definitely are more than just people who have gotten saved.

Let us be glad and rejoice, and give honour to him: for the marriage of the Lamb is come, and his wife hath made herself ready. And to her was granted that she should be arrayed in fine linen, clean and white: for the fine linen is the righteousness of saints. And he saith unto me, Write, Blessed are they which are called unto the marriage supper of the Lamb. And he saith unto me, These are the true sayings of God.   Revelation 19:7-9

It seems clear to me that Jesus, who is the Lamb, will have a Bride, and there will be a Marriage

Supper, a very grand celebration prepared by God Himself.

About thirty years ago a true prophet of God told me something that just makes very good sense. He said that there are three different elements that many preachers do not want to address in a single setting. Jesus will be the Bridegroom, He is the Head of all things. However, many preach that the Church is the Body of Christ. Paul went to great lengths to speak on this subject. Then they will preach a week later that we are also the Bride of Christ. How can we be the Body of Christ and also the Bride of Christ?

The prophet then told me that most of the redeemed will be part of the Body of Christ, but the Bride of Christ must be those within the Body who have loved Jesus more than anything in this world—just as God made a bride for Adam from his side, close to his heart and under his arm. **BOOM!**

I believe I can prove to you that the Bride is not the Body of Christ. The following scriptures clearly tell us who the Bride of Christ is:

> *And there came unto me one of the seven angels which had the seven vials full of the seven last plagues, and talked with me, saying, Come hither, I will shew thee the bride, the Lamb's wife. And he carried me away in the spirit to a great and high mountain, and shewed me that great city, the holy Jerusalem, descending out*

of heaven from God, having the glory of God: and her light
was like unto a stone most precious, even like a jasper stone,
clear as crystal; and had a wall great and high, and had
twelve gates, and at the gates twelve angels, and names
written thereon, which are the names of the twelve tribes of
the children of Israel: on the east three gates; on the north
three gates; on the south three gates; and on the west three
gates. And the wall of the city had twelve foundations, and
in them the names of the twelve apostles of the Lamb.

And he that talked with me had a golden reed to measure the city, and the gates thereof, and the wall thereof.
And the city lieth foursquare, and the length is as large
as the breadth: and he measured the city with the reed,
twelve thousand furlongs. The length and the breadth
and the height of it are equal. And he measured the
wall thereof, an hundred and forty and four cubits, according to the measure of a man, that is, of the angel.
And the building of the wall of it was of jasper: and
the city was pure gold, like unto clear glass. And the
foundations of the wall of the city were garnished with
all manner of precious stones. The first foundation was
jasper; the second, sapphire; the third, a chalcedony;
the fourth, an emerald; the fifth, sardonyx; the sixth,
sardius; the seventh, chrysolyte; the eighth, beryl; the
ninth, a topaz; the tenth, a chrysoprasus; the eleventh,
a jacinth; the twelfth, an amethyst.

And the twelve gates were twelve pearls: every several
gate was of one pearl: and the street of the city was pure

gold, as it were transparent glass. And I saw no temple therein: for the Lord God Almighty and the Lamb are the temple of it. And the city had no need of the sun, neither of the moon, to shine in it: for the glory of God did lighten it, and the Lamb is the light thereof. And the nations of them which are saved shall walk in the light of it: and the kings of the earth do bring their glory and honour into it. And the gates of it shall not be shut at all by day: for there shall be no night there. And they shall bring the glory and honour of the nations into it. And there shall in no wise enter into it any thing that defileth, neither whatsoever worketh abomination, or maketh a lie: but they which are written in the Lamb's book of life. Revelation 21:9-27

Again, verses 9 and 10 say:

And there came unto me one of the seven angels which had the seven vials full of the seven last plagues, and talked with me, saying, Come hither, I will shew thee the bride, the Lamb's wife. And he carried me away in the spirit to a great and high mountain, and shewed me that great city, the holy Jerusalem, descending out of heaven from God.

This says very clearly that the New Jerusalem is the Bride of Christ. Verses 11-27 describe the city in precise detail. It is clear that the Bride of Christ is made up of the occupants of the New Jerusalem. There is not one mention of the Body of Christ here, only the Bride! The prophet reminded me that when John was told to measure the New Jerusalem, it was because it would be occupied by the Bride of Christ. **BOOM!**

God had a plan for the past two thousand years, for the development of a Bride who could rule and reign with His Son, Jesus Christ. Praise God! As I said before, if the powers of darkness had known, they would not have crucified the Christ.

Now we are upon another important threshold. These are the last days, and Jesus will soon come again. Therefore, it behooves us all to learn *How to Be Rapture Ready.*

Chapter 15

Enter John the Baptist
(Elijah)

For several hundred years, the celebration of Passover has had a new tradition implemented in reference to Elijah the prophet. Since the prophet Malachi wrote that Elijah was to come *"before the coming of the great and dreadful day of the Lord,"* the Jewish people, as we have noted, have been leaving an empty seat at their tables with the hope that Elijah would show up at their houses for the Passover meal.

In the New Testament, we read about a priest named Zacharias. He seems to have been an ordinary and fairly insignificant priest, who, according to his time in the rotation of the work schedule, was assigned to serve in the Temple. While working there in the Temple by himself, he was confronted by the same angel that had appeared to Daniel. That's right! The angel Gabriel had returned to look over the setup for the coming of Messiah. The Seed of the woman was to have a forerunner named John, a man who would come *"in the spirit and power of Elias [Elijah]"* (Luke 1:17). Malachi's prophecy was coming to pass. Look at the rest of this amazing story in Luke 1:5-25.

Gabriel informed Zacharias that his wife would soon be having a miracle baby, even though she had never had any children before, she was too old to have children and had been long known as a barren woman. Gabriel also told him that his son was to be called John, which would not be the customary name that should have been given to his son, for that name did not relate to anyone in his family linage.

The angel told Zacharias several other unusual things about his soon-to-be-born son:

*But the angel said unto him, Fear not, Zacharias: for thy prayer is heard; and thy wife Elisabeth shall bear thee a son, and thou shalt call his name John. And thou shalt have joy and gladness; and many shall rejoice at his birth. For he shall be great in the sight of the Lord, and shall drink neither wine nor strong drink; and **he shall be filled with the Holy Ghost, even from his mother's womb**. And many of the children of Israel shall he turn to the Lord their God. And he shall go before him **in the spirit and power of Elias, to turn the hearts of the fathers to the children, and the disobedient to the wisdom of the just**; to make ready a people prepared for the Lord.* Luke 1:13-17

There it is, the setup by God's direction, sending Gabriel to make the announcement of John's birth. His assignment would be to turn the hearts of the fathers to the children. If he could not do that, God would smite the earth with a curse. The accomplishment of the assignment was dependent upon the receptivity of the people.

Let's refer again to Malachi 4:6, the last verse in the Old Testament:

And he shall turn the heart of the fathers to the children, and the heart of the children to their fathers, lest I come and smite the earth with a curse.

It was not the responsibility of John to turn the fathers' or children's hearts. His responsibility was to go before the Lord God (the Messiah) as the forerunner and to declare His coming. Elijah was coming, and he would be filled with the Holy Ghost from his mother's womb.

And what was John's message?

And as the people were in expectation, and all men mused in their hearts of John, whether he were the Christ, or not; John answered, saying unto them all, I indeed baptize you with water; but one mightier than I cometh, the latchet of whose shoes I am not worthy to unloose: he shall baptize you with the Holy Ghost and with fire: whose fan is in his hand, and he will throughly purge his floor, and will gather the wheat into his garner; but the chaff he will burn with fire unquenchable. And many other things in his exhortation preached he unto the people.   Luke 3:15-18

John preached repentance, and he baptized the people with a baptism of repentance. His message was strong. He openly proclaimed that he was *not* the Messiah, but that when Messiah would come, He would baptize the people with the Holy Ghost and fire. John's ministry grew. Then Jesus, before He was revealed as the Messiah, came to the area where John was baptizing the people in the Jordan River. John looked up and saw his cousin coming at a distance and began to speak forth two very important prophetic utterances:

1.) *"Behold the Lamb of God!"*
2.) *"Which taketh away the sin of the world."*
                                      John 1:29

These profound announcements, that Jesus was the Lamb of God, and that He takes away the sin of the world, had never been declared before. Sins were never ever taken away under the Old Covenant. They were only covered by the shedding of the blood of bulls and goats. John was announcing to the world that the sins of the world would no longer simply be covered, but instead, would be taken away in Chirst.

Jeremiah declared:

And they shall teach no more every man his neighbour, and every man his brother, saying, Know the LORD: for they shall all know me, from the least of them unto the greatest of them, saith the LORD: for I will forgive their iniquity, and I will remember their sin no more. Jeremiah 31:34

The psalmist declared:

As far as the east is from the west, so far hath he removed our transgressions from us. Psalm 103:12

Also, the announcement that Jesus was the Lamb of God was a declaration that He was indeed the Messiah. After centuries of waiting for Him, Messiah had not only been born into the world; He was standing there as a thirty-year-old man in the midst of the people.

If that was not enough, Jesus asked John to baptize Him, and soon the heavens would open, and Father God would confirm Jesus as His Son:

And Jesus, when he was baptized, went up straightway out of the water: and, lo, the heavens were opened unto him, and he saw the Spirit of God descending like a dove, and lighting upon him: and lo a voice from heaven, saying, This is my beloved Son, in whom I am well pleased. Matthew 3:16-17

The Old Testament prophets had foretold a day when the people's sins would no longer be remembered against them. They talked about a time coming in which our transgressions would be separated from us *"as far as the east is from the west,"* (Psalm 103:12). At the time, no one had yet experienced anything like that and therefore they could not possibly conceive of what that would be like.

King David got close to the understanding of this coming miracle, when he cried out to God in prayer:

Create in me a clean heart, O God; and renew a right spirit within me. Cast me not away from thy presence; and take not thy Holy Spirit from me.
Psalm 51:10-11

The Holy Spirit had only come *upon* David, but was not allowed to come *into* him. You and I are blessed to live in the day of the fulfillment of these prophecies. Personally, I cannot understand how people can reject the complete experience of the Baptism of the Holy Spirit. The precious infilling of the Holy Spirit is wonderful. I treasure it.

All too soon, the life of John the Baptist (Elijah come in spirit and power) was cut short, and he died a martyr. His work had been to pave the way for Jesus, and he did that well. That he died prematurely is a subject for another book. Our focus here is what is happening in our world today, the struggle of Satan against the DNA of mankind. You and I must learn, and quickly, *How to Be Rapture Ready*.

CHAPTER 16

ENTER JESUS, THE SEED OF THE WOMAN

As the centuries passed, God hovered over His Word to bring to pass this most important moment in history. Satan, with all of his feverish working, would not be successful in blocking the coming of the Seed of the woman. He wasn't about to give up, however.

When the time was right, God once again sent the archangel Gabriel, this time to announce the Child's birth to the woman He had selected as the worthy vessel. She was Mary, a citizen of Nazareth, a woman who was espoused (to a man named Joseph), but who was yet a virgin. The battle of the ages was in full sway.

Before Jesus was born, Mary visited her cousin Elisabeth, who was pregnant with John (who would be known as the Baptist). The presence of God on Mary caused both Elisabeth and John to be filled with the Holy Ghost.

The angel of the Lord foretold to Zacharias that his wife Elisabeth would have a child named John.

In Luke 1:15, the angel told Zacharias that their baby would be filled with the Holy Ghost, even from his mother's womb.

The fulfillment of the angel's prophecy came to pass in Luke 1:41, when the baby leaped in Elisabeth's womb, and she was filled with the Holy Ghost. Later, on, in Luke 1:67, it is clear that Zacharias was also filled with the Holy Ghost and began to prophesy.

Angels sang at Christ's birth and prophecy was fulfilled, for, oddly enough, He was born in Bethlehem. Herod was asked by some visiting Magi, *"Where is he that is born King of the Jews?"* (Matthew 2:2). They had seen His star in the east and had come to worship Him. Even heathen magi recognized His coming.

Satan was scrambling now to destroy "the Seed of the woman." But in spite of everything Satan could do, God's Son was circumcised and dedicated in the Temple, and, there again, profound prophecies were spoken over His life. In this way, God successfully slipped His Son into the world, the greatest Secret of all time, right under Satan's nose.

Since God had to keep this Seed protected, Jesus had to be hidden until the day of His revealing. Therefore, God sent an angel to enter the dream of Joseph and tell him to take the child and flee to Egypt. Herod was seeking the Child, to take His life. Then, after a few years, God sent Gabriel in another dream, this one in Egypt, to tell Joseph to take Mary and Jesus and return to Israel.

Although not much is known of Jesus' childhood, at twelve years of age, He confounded the doctors in the Temple with His depth of knowledge of the holy books. In addition, as we can see from the genealogy of Christ in the books of Luke and Matthew, both Mary and Joseph were of pure DNA all the way back to Adam.

Satan did not know where Jesus was, but the Seed of the woman was alive and well, and, as the Scriptures so aptly describe, He was growing *"in wisdom and stature, and in favour with God and man"* (Luke 2:52).

BE AT PEACE! BE NOT AFRAID!

Trust me, we do not have to worry about the elites of this world taking over, because, until the Rapture takes place, Holy Spirit-filled people are hindering this takeover by the Antichrist, as revealed in 2 Thessalonians 2:7:

For the mystery of iniquity doth already work: only he who now letteth will let, until he be taken out of the way.

The Greek word translated here as *let* means "hinder." In other words, he that hinders will hinder until he is taken out of the way. True Christians are hindering Satan from establishing a one-world government

141

on the Earth. I believe God placed President Donald Trump into office to slow the premature push to bring Satan's one-world government and globalism and, thus, usher the Antichrist into a position of power.

Even after the Rapture of the Church, God will bring His two candlesticks, the two witnesses spoken of in Revelation 11:3, into the streets of Jerusalem, and all the power of military might will not be able to remove them.

Rumors of the Defense Advanced Research Projects Agency controlling our weather, chem trails taking over our bodies, the NSA recording every phone call in the world, or GPS surveillance and tracking of a person's every move do not matter. God said:

He that sitteth in the heavens shall laugh: the LORD shall have them in derision.   Psalm 2:4

God can still hold the world's elites hostage and at bay by simply letting fire come from His two witnesses. That fire will kill anyone who tries to stop them from preaching. Then, when the enemies of God finally kill these two men, they will be helpless to remove their dead bodies from the streets. On the third day, they will be raised from the dead and will ascend into Heaven as the whole world watches it all play out on live television.

I am convinced that the Coronavirus Pandemic was a ploy used by Satan to prematurely usher in the one-world order. It is already failing, and I believe God will use it to begin the greatest revival in the history of the world. However, those in charge of this world's systems *will* try to use the Pandemic to promote the collection of everyone's DNA.

I prophesy to you, not by the Word of the Lord, but from what I see in the Word of God, that Donald J. Trump or a person of like spirit (someone who is anti-Globalism, anti-New World Order and very much pro-Israel, will be re-elected. Within a short period of time, this new president will give the leadership of Israel a promise that they can build the final Temple on the Temple Mount. I say this because the angel of the Lord told John in Revelation 11:2 to measure the temple but not the courtyard. God said through the angel that the courtyard had been given to the Gentiles! **BOOM!**

Remember, every U.S. resident for more than twenty-four years said that he would move the U.S. Embassy to Jerusalem (the Jewish capital), but each time, because the Arab world threatened that if it happened, there would be 500,000 Arabs in the streets of Jerusalem demonstrating, no president had the fortitude to keep their word! When Donald J. Trump made the decision to move our embassy, instantly everything fell into place, and it was done in less that six months!

I believe that when the next Trump-like president tells Israel that he will protect them from the Muslim world, they will begin construction of the Temple within a very few months. All is in readiness. The Al-Aqsa Mosque can stay where it is, and there will still be plenty of room on the Temple Mount for the new Temple. Time is running out, but the end is not yet! Hold firm to your faith! Occupy until the Rapture. Remember what the Scriptures say:

> *He that sitteth in the heavens shall laugh: the Lord shall have them in derision.*   Romans 8:14

BOOM!

Be led by the Holy Spirit! He is within you! God always gets the last word. Just make sure you know *How to Be Rapture Ready*.

CHAPTER 17

NOW, ABOUT THE RAPTURE OF THE CHURCH

In the previous chapters, I have presented what I believe is conclusive scriptural evidence for the premise that the battle of the ages is over the destruction of the DNA of humankind. Now, let us consider the final battle of the ages: Satan's plan to destroy man's belief in God and his belief in the Rapture of those *"that love His appearing"* (2 Timothy 4:8).

Jesus asked the question:

> *Nevertheless, when the Son of man cometh, shall he find faith on the earth?* Luke 18:8

This question begs an answer. When the Son of man comes (that's the Rapture), will He find faith in God, faith in His Word. God sent His Comforter, the Holy Spirit, as the earnest of our inheritance, the down payment on our relationship, and all that God has in store for those who are looking for Him and those who love His appearing. Paul wrote to the Ephesians:

Having made known unto us the mystery of his will, according to his good pleasure which he hath purposed in himself: that in the dispensation of the fulness of times he might gather together in one all things in Christ, both which are in heaven, and which are on earth; even in him: in whom also we have obtained an inheritance, being predestinated according to the purpose of him who worketh all things after the counsel of his own will: that we should be to the praise of his glory, who first trusted in Christ. In whom ye also trusted, after that ye heard the word of truth, the gospel of your salvation: in whom also after that ye believed, ye were sealed with that holy Spirit of promise, which is the earnest of our inheritance until the redemption of the purchased possession, unto the praise of his glory.

Ephesians 1:9-14

Notice especially verse 14:

Which is the earnest of our inheritance until the redemption of the purchased possession, unto the praise of his glory.

When the Holy Spirit was sent to Earth in His fullness on the Day of Pentecost, He was the *"earnest,"* the guarantee or down payment of our inheritance until the finalization of our redemption. There will be a finalization. Jesus is coming for those who love His appearing and are watching for Him.

Paul wrote to Timothy:

Henceforth there is laid up for me a crown of righteousness, which the Lord, the righteous judge, shall give me at that day: and not to me only, but unto all them also that love his appearing.   2 Timothy 4:8

Jesus Himself stated:

But rather seek ye the kingdom of God; and all these things shall be added unto you.
Fear not, little flock; for it is your Father's good pleasure to give you the kingdom. Sell that ye have, and give alms; provide yourselves bags which wax not old, a treasure in the heavens that faileth not, where no thief approacheth, neither moth corrupteth. For where your treasure is, there will your heart be also.
Let your loins be girded about, and your lights burning; and ye yourselves like unto men that wait for their lord, when he will return from the wedding; that when he cometh and knocketh, they may open unto him immediately. Blessed are those servants, whom the lord when he cometh shall find watching: verily I say unto you, that he shall gird himself, and make them to sit

down to meat, and will come forth and serve them. And if he shall come in the second watch, or come in the third watch, and find them so, blessed are those servants.

Luke 12:31-38

This takes us back to what Malachi said just before he spoke of the *"curse"* coming if mankind rejected the coming of Elijah (see Malachi 4:5-6). He also said:

Then they that feared the LORD spake often one to another: and the LORD hearkened, and heard it, and a book of remembrance was written before him for them that feared the LORD, and that thought upon his name. And they shall be mine, saith the LORD of hosts, in that day when I make up my jewels; and I will spare them, as a man spareth his own son that serveth him.

Malachi 3:16-17

Notice that we are God's jewels. He is coming for us, and we will be spared when He comes *"as a man spares his own son."* This could not be more clear. We have been put illegally in a place that our Owner did not put us. One day He will come to reclaim the jewels that belong to Him. Praise God! **BOOM!**
Notice what Paul wrote to the Thessalonians:

But of the times and the seasons, brethren, ye have no need that I write unto you. For yourselves know *perfectly that the day of the Lord so cometh as a thief in the night. For when **they** shall say, Peace and safety; then sudden destruction cometh upon **them**, as travail upon a woman with child; and **they** shall not escape. But **ye**, brethren, are not in darkness, that that day should overtake **you** as a thief. **Ye** are all the children of light, and the children of the day: **we** are not of the night, nor of darkness.*   1 Thessalonians 5:1-5

He clearly states in these verses that <u>Jesus is not coming for us *"as a thief."*</u> The adjectives here are *"they"* and *"them,"* not *"ye"* and *"you."* *"They"* will not escape. <u>He is coming as a thief in the night for *"them,"* not for **you**.</u> **BOOM!**

When Jesus comes for us, it will be to take away those who think on His name. He is coming for His jewels, those who have been oppressed by Satan and who have been illegally made to believe that Satan has authority over the redeemed!

Once again, notice the wording in Malachi 3. The Lord says that He is coming for those who think on His name:

Then they that feared the Lord spake often one to another: and the Lord hearkened, and heard it, and a book of remembrance was written before him for them that feared the Lord, and that thought upon his name. And they shall be mine, saith the Lord of hosts, in that day when I make up my jewels; and I will spare them, as a man spareth his own son that serveth him. Then shall ye return, and discern between the righteous and the wicked, between him that serveth God and him that serveth him not. Malachi 3:16-18

Consider the following scriptures spoken by Jesus:

But know this, that if the goodman of the house had known in what watch the thief would come, he would have watched, and would not have suffered his house to be broken up. Matthew 24:43

And this know, that if the goodman of the house had known what hour the thief would come, he would have watched, and not have suffered his house to be broken through. Be ye therefore ready also: for the Son of man cometh at an hour when ye think not. Luke 12:39-40

This may sound confusing, but let me sort it out for you. In this parable, *"the goodman of the house"* is Satan, and the thief is Jesus Christ. Jesus is speaking a parable about Himself coming into a house and stealing jewels from the one who has possession of them unjustly. In this case, the jewels belong to Jesus, and He comes in the night to rescue those jewels that are rightfully His.

This is *"the dreadful day of the LORD"* referred to in Malachi 4:5. It will indeed be dreadful for Satan and all who are left behind. Can you imagine people coming to the conclusion that Jesus has come, and they have been left behind?

By the Holy Spirit, Paul expounded in the New Testament on what he had read about in the book of Isaiah:

For since the beginning of the world men have not heard, nor perceived by the ear, neither hath the eye seen, O God, beside thee, what he hath prepared for him that waiteth for him. Isaiah 64:4

Here's what he wrote to the Corinthians:

But we speak the wisdom of God in a mystery, even the hidden wisdom, which God ordained before the world unto our glory: which none of the princes of this world knew: for had they known it, they would not have crucified the Lord of glory. But as it is written,

> *Eye hath not seen, nor ear heard, neither have entered into the heart of man, the things which God hath prepared for them that love him.*

But God hath revealed them unto us by his Spirit: for the Spirit searcheth all things, yea, the deep things of God. For what man knoweth the things of a man, save the spirit of man which is in him? even so the things of God knoweth no man, but the Spirit of God. Now we have received, not the spirit of the world, but the spirit which is of God; that we might know the things that are freely given to us of God.

1 Corinthians 2:7-12

What does it all mean? Jesus is coming for those who love Him. The Rapture is real, and you and I need to be sure we know *How to Be Rapture Ready.*

CHAPTER 18

TERMS USED REGARDING THE RAPTURE

There is nothing in the Word of God that would designate that all the terms used to describe the Rapture must happen in less than a second of time. I believe that the terms used to describe the Rapture are descriptions of events that will take place during *"the Day of the LORD."*

As you may know, the word *rapture* does not appear in the Bible. There are, however, five terms used in the New Testament regarding the Rapture. They are:

His Coming
Being Taken
The Gathering
The Change
The Catching Away

These terms are each totally different from the others and do not have to be happening all at the same time. Let us see what the Word of God says regarding the use of each of these terms:

1. HIS COMING

For as the lightning cometh out of the east, and shineth even unto the west; so shall also the coming of the Son of man be.   Matthew 24:27

From this, we learn that Christ's coming will be like lightening, sudden, without warning, without us knowing exactly when or where it will come.

But as the days of Noe were, so shall also the coming of the Son of man be ... .
And knew not until the flood came, and took them all away; so shall also the coming of the Son of man be.
                              Matthew 24:37 and 39

In the days of Noah, God suddenly shut the door of the ark, but there was not a sudden disappearance of the ark itself.

2. BEING TAKEN

I tell you, in that night there shall be two men in one bed; the one shall be taken, and the other shall be left. Two women shall be grinding together; the one shall be taken, *and the other left. Two men shall be in the field; the one <u>shall be taken</u>, and the other left.*   Luke 17: 34-36

According to *Strong's Concordance* the Greek word used here is *paralambano*. It has the *Strong's* designated number of G3880. This word is defined as follows: "1.) to take to, to take with one's self, to join with one's self an associate, a companion." Some have defined the word as meaning "drawn to one's side in a loving manner."

Incredibly, in John 14:3, the word *receive* is translated from this same Greek word—*paralambano*! Pay attention to the exact wording, and you will have a greater understanding of a word that describes a part of the Rapture.

And if I go and prepare a place for you, I will come again, and receive you unto myself; that where I am, there ye may be also.   John 14:3

3. THE GATHERING

Now we beseech you, brethren, by the coming of our Lord Jesus Christ, and by our gathering together unto him ... .   2 Thessalonians 2:1

It seems that the *coming* of the Lord and the *gathering* together unto Him could very well be two closely related, but separate, events. This word *gathering* is translated from the Greek word *episynagoge*. This is shown in the *Strong's Concordance* as number 1997. It is translated into English only two times: once as *gathering together* and the other time as *assembling together,* as found in the book of Hebrews:

Not forsaking the assembling of ourselves together, as the manner of some is; but exhorting one another: and so much the more, as ye see the day approaching.
Hebrews 10:25

I find it quite interesting that the word *synagogue* is in this Hebrew word. To me, this makes the definition very clear. *Strong's* defines this word as "1.) a gathering together in one place 2.) the (religious) assembly (of Christians)."

4. The Change

Behold, I shew you a mystery; We shall not all sleep, but we shall all be changed, in a moment, in the twinkling of an eye, at the last trump: for the trumpet shall sound, and the dead shall be raised incorruptible, and we shall be changed. For this corruptible must put on incorruption, and this mortal must put on immortality.
1 Corinthians 15:51-53

This word *changed* is translated from the Greek word *allasso*. In *Strong's*, it is designated by the number 236 and has the definition "to make different: change." This speaks of those who are living when Christ returns.

Paul wrote that the dead in Christ will be raised first, and then those believers who are still alive at Christ's return will be changed:

For the Lord himself shall descend from heaven with a shout, with the voice of the archangel, and with the trump of God: and the dead in Christ shall rise first: then we which are alive and remain shall be caught up together with them in the clouds, to meet the Lord in the air: and so shall we ever be with the Lord.

1 Thessalonians 4:16-17

If the dead in Christ rise first, and then those who are alive are caught up, these events do not necessarily happen all at once, in a single instant!

5. THE CATCHING AWAY

Then we which are alive and remain shall be caught up together with them in the clouds, to meet the Lord in the air: and so shall we ever be with the Lord.

1 Thessalonians 4:17

The word that is translated *caught up* is the Greek word *harpazo*. In *Strong's*, it is designated by the number 726 and has the definition "to seize (in various applications): catch (away, up) pluck, pull, take (by force)." I believe we get our English word *harpoon* from this word, as it describes the very action the Greek word implies. This was the word used to describe the "catching away" of Philip after he baptized the eunuch in water in Acts 8:39. The apostle Paul used this same word in 2 Corinthians 12:2 and 4 when describing his being "caught up" into the third Heaven. His experience was so profound that he could not tell if he was in his body or out of his body.

In conclusion, there can be no doubt. The Bible teaches the Rapture. Whatever we choose to call it, the important thing is that we are assured of *How to Be Rapture Ready*.

WHAT JESUS TAUGHT REGARDING THE RAPTURE

In Luke 17, Jesus said many exceptional things regarding the Rapture of the Church. I want to begin with verse 26.

And as it was in the days of Noe, so shall it be also in the days of the Son of man.　　　　　Luke 17:26

I will only do a recap here of the main things that this verse speaks to, since the first part of the book goes into incredible detail concerning the days of Noah from Genesis 6. I want to paraphrase what Jesus said here in Luke 17:26-27:

As it was in the days of Noah, so shall it be in the days of the Son of man. They were marrying and giving in marriage until the day Noah entered into the ark and the flood came.

Genesis 6 states that there were giants in the land in those days because the fallen angels were intermarrying with the human race. The DNA of these men and women was, therefore, tainted.

As was noted earlier in the book, this happened because of what God said in Genesis 3:15. The man and the woman were tricked by Satan and fell into the sin of disobedience. Therefore, God said, the Seed of the woman would bruise the head of Satan. Immediately, Satan began to seek to destroy the Seed of the woman by mixing the seed of fallen angels with the human race, so that the Word of God could not come to pass.

By Genesis 6, just three chapters after God prophesied the destruction of Satan, the enemy had already contaminated much of the DNA of mankind. As I have already presented, this was the beginning of the battle of the ages, an effort to tamper with the DNA of the human race and, thus, protect Satan from everlasting damnation.

Noah, you might remember, was chosen by God to preserve the human race. His DNA was pure all the way back to Adam. It was not that he was so holy, but that his DNA was not tainted by the fallen angels.

Jesus came to redeem mankind. He was not (and is not) a being who was part man and part angel. He was the perfect, sinless Son of God. The Bible was written to tell the story of the redemption of mankind, who was made in the image of God and after His likeness.

When Jesus comes back to rapture the redeemed of mankind, it will be at a time when the DNA of mankind is being tampered with again. As it was in the days of Noah, today scientists are tampering with our DNA again. Who can deny that we are living in the days in which our DNA is being researched to make it possible to integrate artificial intelligence with the human body?

Jesus warned, *"As it was in the days of Noe,"* *"as it was in the days of Lot,"* and *"Remember Lot's wife"*:

And as it was in the days of Noe, so shall it be also in the days of the Son of man. They did eat, they drank, they married wives, they were given in marriage, until the day that Noe entered into the ark, and the flood came, and destroyed them all.

Likewise also as it was in the days of Lot; they did eat, they drank, they bought, they sold, they planted, they builded; but the same day that Lot went out of Sodom it rained fire and brimstone from heaven, and destroyed them all.

Even thus shall it be in the day when the Son of man is revealed. In that day, he which shall be upon the housetop, and his stuff in the house, let him not come down to take it away: and he that is in the field, let him likewise not return back. Remember Lot's wife.

Whosoever shall seek to save his life shall lose it; and whosoever shall lose his life shall preserve it. I tell you, in that night there shall be two men in one bed; the one shall be taken, and the other shall be left. Two women shall be grinding together; the one shall be taken, and the other left. Two men shall be in the field; the one shall be taken, and the other left.

And they answered and said unto him, Where, Lord? And he said unto them, Wheresoever the body is, thither will the eagles be gathered together.

Luke 17:26-37

In these verses, we are reminded of Lot and his family. If you will recall, angels were sent by God to rescue Lot and his family from Sodom. The problem was that although they were vexed by the sins of that city, they didn't really want to leave it. Lot was so compromised that he even offered his daughters to be ravished by the perverted men of Sodom to protect the angels. And it is like that today. Even Christians are compromised and vexed by the pleasures of the sin of our day.

I believe that it is very possible that angels will be sent by God to announce that they will take us to a Rapture place to get us out of this world before the Antichrist takes over with his one-world government. However, multitudes of Christians may very well resist their moment of exit because they have been taught that when the Rapture takes place, they will just "poof" out of here. Cars will crash, planes will fall out of the sky, and chaos and confusion will be the order of the day. But God is not the author of confusion. Everything God does will be decent and in order.

Consider what Jesus taught here about Lot and his family. If Christians were just going to "poof" out of the Earth, Jesus would not have said in verse 31: *"In that day, he which shall be upon his housetop, and his stuff in the house, let him not come down to take it away: and he that is in the field, let him likewise not return back,"* and, again, in verse 32, *"Remember Lot's wife!"* **BOOM!**

Luke 17:31-32 makes it clear that this event is not instantaneous or else Jesus would not be telling us to compare this event to Lot's experience. It took time for the angels to get Lot's family out of Sodom. Even when Lot's wife was taken out of Sodom, she had time to think about it, and, unfortunately, she did not make it all the way to safety. She looked back and lost her moment of rescue. The warning is this: if we are upon the housetop with our stuff in the house, we should not come down to get it. He that is in the field, let him likewise not return back. The implication here is to not go back into the house to get your "stuff."

The Rapture is not going to be a cakewalk, but it actually may be the biggest test of our faith. When you read Hebrew 11, often called the faith chapter, it becomes apparent that everything that was done in the Old Testament was done *"by faith,"* for example:

By faith Enoch was translated.   Hebrews 11:5

Without faith it is impossible to please him [God].
                                                        Hebrews 11:6

Everything in God requires faith. Jesus said:

Whosoever shall seek to save his life shall lose it; and whosoever shall lose his life shall preserve it.
                                                        Luke 17:33

Also, consider these words by Jesus:

I tell you, in that night there shall be two men in one bed; the one shall be taken, and the other shall be left. Two women shall be grinding together; the one shall be taken, and the other left. Two men shall be in the field; the one shall be taken, and the other left.   Luke 17:34-36

In the same context of the angels taking Lot and his family out of Sodom, Jesus continued to teach that one person will be taken and another left. This inspired the disciples to ask Him a question that I've never heard any Bible scholar address in a satisfactory way. These disciples knew that He was referring to a location, so in the first part of verse 37, they asked Him the all-important question:

> *And they answered and said unto him, Where, Lord? And he said unto them, Wheresoever the body is, thither will the eagles be gathered together.*
>
> Luke 17:37

"Where, Lord?" was the question, and the answer was profound, confusing and very unusual. Jesus said, *"Wheresoever the body is, thither [there] will the eagles be gathered together."* But what does that mean?

This word *body* is translated from the Greek word *soma* (*Strong's* G4983, #963; #8182; #956; #945; transliteration, neuter noun, root word (etymology) from #963; #8180; #950; #969; G4982). The definition is "the body both of men or animals, a dead body or corpse." **BOOM!**

Jesus was saying that where they were being taken was a place where dead bodies would be. I can only conclude that at the Rapture place there will be dead bodies because all who try to insert themselves into the Rapture event will be slain on the spot. I believe that the Antichrist, who will swiftly come to full power directly after this Rapture event, will explain to the world that multitudes were found dead around thousands of churches. He will explain away all the deaths by saying that these must have been radical religious people who committed suicide.

165

The press will not allow much discussion regarding the missing people who went up in the Rapture, as they will consider the world to be better off without them. After all, they opposed the one-world society. They were therefore considered to be selfish and racist.

The press will also write off the disappearances of so many people by saying they were possible alien abductions by the UFOs that have been seen so much in recent years. Fallen angel encounters will also be reported as the time draws closer because Satan will be desperate to sow confusion into the hearts of mankind. Remember what the Word of God says:

If it were possible, they shall deceive the very elect.
Matthew 24:24

Just as Lot's wife was taken out of Sodom to be delivered from the coming destruction, but was smitten dead and became a pillar of salt, could it be that on the day of the Rapture many people, who might otherwise be saved, will be lukewarm and love the world more than they love the Lord and refuse to go in the Rapture? The implication is clear.

Jesus also said:

Not every one that saith unto me, Lord, Lord, shall enter into the kingdom of heaven; but he that doeth the will of my Father which is in heaven.   Matthew 7:21

Wow! Christians will be left behind in the Rapture because they have no desire to go with Jesus. That's a wake-up call, isn't it? The Rapture is real, and you and I must be ready for it. Do whatever it takes to learn *How to Be Rapture Ready.*

CHAPTER 20

THE END OF THE BOOK REPEATED

This is the last chapter of the book. I repeated it at the beginning for effect. I am confident that if you have read the entire book, you will now totally understand this final chapter. This is only a scenario of how the events of the Rapture *might* take place. The scenario covers the greatest event of all times and includes the major concepts that Christians everywhere have referred to and have believed regarding the Rapture of the Church. All throughout the Bible you have seen that this Rapture event is referred to as *"the Day of the Lord."*

I pray that reading the book thus far has blessed you and will cause faith to rise in your heart, faith that the Rapture is real. Most importantly, I pray that no matter how the Rapture takes place, you will be ready for this event and not be left behind!

Now, again, here is how our scenario plays out:

A man and his wife are in their house. It is an ordinary day, during a time when the whole world is under great pressure and change. Confusion and unrest are prevalent all over the world. It is difficult to go through daily activities because of shortages and distresses. There have been upheavals around the globe. Politicians seem to be incapable of making peace among the nations. The great nations of the world have declined in influence. The economies of the world are in disarray. The latest nuclear exchanges between the most powerful nations of the Earth, though limited in scope, have made it clear that "peace through strength" can no longer work. The people of the whole world and the news organizations of the world seem fixated on one and only one issue: Who can make peace? Is there not *someone* who can bring peace to the world?

There is much talk about a certain politician from the Middle East who seems to have a message that could appease all groups of religious leaders, especially Muslims and Jews. He is a powerful and charismatic person, and religious leaders have announced that they would put their influence behind him so peace can come once again on Earth.

The wife speaks:

"As I was entering into the room where my husband was watching the news, I was contemplating these things and thinking that it was only last Sunday I heard a sermon about praying that the Lord would *'come quickly.'* While musing about this, I heard a very loud sound coming from outside my house. It sounded like a loud horn that could possibly be a new alarm system that the city might have installed to alert us about problems with the local chemical plants on the other side of town. I said to my husband, 'Dear, what is that loud-sounding horn that I just heard blaring outside?' I was puzzled when he replied, 'I didn't hear any loud sound. What are you talking about?'

"Before I could respond to my husband, a man suddenly appeared in the room before me. I was overwhelmed by a knowing that he was an angel. I was puzzled in my mind, as he greeted me by my name. Amazingly, my husband apparently could not see him. This being that appeared to me began to say, 'Be not afraid. I have come to take you to a certain church where the Rapture is taking place.'

"It was then I remembered that the Bible says to *try the spirits* to see if they are of God. I blurted out, 'Did Jesus Christ come in the flesh?' At the same moment I was hearing the angel's response, I heard my husband ask, 'Who are you talking to, dear? Are you crazy?' It seemed like my husband was far away in the background, but I heard the angel clearly saying, 'Of course, Jesus Christ came in the flesh. Now, let's go!'

"At that moment, I remembered hearing about a minister from the East Coast of the United States talking about how the Rapture was always called, 'The Day of the Lord,' not a 'poofing out of the Earth.' I also remembered the minister saying that Jesus warned us, *"Remember Lot's wife"* and that the Rapture could be the biggest test of a person's faith. He mentioned that the angels came and took Lot's family, including his wife, out of the city of Sodom. I remembered that pastor also saying that Jesus said, *'If you are in the field, do not go back to your house.'* The pastor also said, 'When the angel comes to take you to the place of the Rapture, you should not hesitate. Nor should you delay going with the angel because you may want to check on your children to make sure they are saved. If you delay, the angel will say, 'Do as you will; I have to go now.'

"I turned to my husband and said to him, 'An angel has appeared in the room and told me I must go with him now to a certain local church because the Rapture is taking place.' My husband's impassioned response was, 'I forbid you to go with whomever you say has appeared to you!'

"Again, I remembered the pastor's sermon in which he said that the Rapture might be the greatest test of a Christians' faith. He had emphasized Luke 17, which states, *'If you are on the top of your house, do not go back down into your house. If you are in the field, do not go back to your house. One shall be taken, the other left.'* He said,

'On the day of the Rapture, do not delay to try to check on your children or loved ones. Go immediately with the angel of the Lord! Do not let anything hinder you.' He had talked about where Luke 17 says, *'Remember Lot's wife.'*

"As I was leaving through the door with the angel, I blurted out to my husband, 'I have been a good wife to you all these years, but this time I must leave because I am not going to miss out on the Rapture.' For a fleeting moment, I thought that my husband would try to follow me to the church where the angel was taking me.

"As I was stepping off the front porch of my house, an amazing thing happened. It was as if my spirit and soul was in overdrive. My mind seemed to be unlocked, and I was able to clearly process details faster than the speed of light. I had been translated, and instantly the angel and I were at the church more than five miles away. I was puzzled that, in a fraction of a second, I had traveled more than five miles.

"Descending from above the church to the entrance, I saw what appeared to be people lying on the ground as if they were dead. It was not like me, but I was not afraid. I was at perfect peace that this was all part of the Rapture. Being filled with confidence, yet overwhelmed by my new-found ability to process the magnitude of information in microseconds, I found myself at the entrance of the church.

"As I stepped inside the church, I saw more than a thousand people sitting there. At the front of this great church, I saw what I instinctively knew was a large angel dressed like a man. He was standing behind the podium with a large book in front of him. I became aware of a conversation the angel in charge was having with a man sitting just a few rows behind me. I heard the angel saying, 'Why are you here without your robe of righteousness on?' The man did not answer for a period of time. He seemed to be speechless. Then the angel in charge said to the ushers, *'Bind him hand and foot, and take him away, and cast him into outer darkness; there shall be weeping and gnashing of teeth.'* Somehow, without knowing how, I knew the reference was from Matthew 22:1-14, which is The Parable of the Gathering. It was then that I understood where some of the bodies outside had come from and that the people lying there were indeed dead.

"I remembered the pastor preaching that Jesus said, *'One shall be taken and the other left.'* The disciples asked Him in Luke 17:37, *'Taken where, Lord?'* His response has almost never been understood nor addressed by pastors. Jesus answered, *'Where the dead bodies are there will the eagles be gathered.'* Supernaturally, I had a complete understanding of this verse, and I became aware that, during the Rapture, many will overhear what is happening and seek to push themselves into the event without being invited. The judgement of God will fall on them, and they will be slain on the spot.

"It was then that I saw the pastor of the church come through the side door. He asked the angel in charge, 'What is going on?' The angel calmly, but sternly told the pastor that he should take a seat, as the Rapture was taking place. The pastor seemed bewildered. He asked the angel what gave him the right to take over this church? The angel in charge simply informed the pastor that on May 8, 1958, the church members, along with the pastor at that time, had dedicated the property and the buildings to the Lord Jesus Christ. The angel explained that the Lord Himself had now authorized this place as one of many locations that would be used as Rapture points. With that being settled, the angel in charge continued.

"I sat there in amazement as the angel called out people seated in the auditorium one by one. Then I saw the angel point at me, and I heard him ask, 'What is your name?' In fear and trembling, I answered him and told him my name. Instantly, the leaves of the book in front of him began to turn, as if by unseen hands. The angel spoke in a strong voice that could be heard all over the auditorium. It sounded as if it had been amplified, but the PA system was not turned on. He replied to me, 'Yes, your name is in the book. Come forward up the steps to the platform.' Enveloped in the awesome presence of the Lord, I approached the angel. As I walked up the steps to the top of the platform, I noticed that every fiber of my being had begun to vibrate. When I reached the top of the steps, the angel lifted his right arm, fully extended, and said, 'Well done! Enter into the joy of the Lord!'

"As I walked under his extended arm, I noticed that I was walking about a foot above the platform. A brilliant light was shining out from my body. Then, to my shock, my body began to change in a moment, in the twinkling of an eye. My clothes were falling to the platform, but my nakedness could not be seen. I was clothed in the glory of God. It happened so fast that I could barely comprehend all that was taking place.

"When I looked up, the back of the church appeared to be open, even though I knew it was enclosed in the building structure. My supernatural eyes had been opened, and I could see through the wall. Beyond the wall there was a large chariot full of people who, like me, had been changed. They were rejoicing, crying out for joy and shouting praises to God in such a glorious and beautiful way and with a volume I had never heard on Earth before.

"I started rejoicing with them and ran on air through that back wall so fast, knowing that I had been taken by an angel to the gathering place. There I had been changed and was on my way to be carried to Heaven in a magnificent chariot, just like Elijah.

As I was getting into the chariot, I glanced over to my right and noticed the husband of my earthly life was one of those lying on the ground. He must have driven to the church to get me, but that fleeting thought could not dampen my joy. I had made it into the chariot, and I was going to my true home in Heaven, to be with my Lord."

Okay, now you have read the last chapter of the book again. Let me remind you that this scenario may not be exactly the way everything happens, but one thing is for sure: Christ's coming will be sudden, and we must be ready no matter how it happens, to make sure we do not miss it. If we have predetermined mind-sets as to how it will all take place, we might resist the actual way Jesus comes and miss the greatest event of all ages. My goal has been to bring you into an understanding of how the Rapture may take place and help you to know *How to Be Rapture Ready*!

CHAPTER 21

IN CLOSING

In closing, there are four parables I wish to address that you can use to challenge your readiness for the Rapture. Many might say that these parables do not apply to the Rapture of the Church. I believe that as you read them and meditate on them, you will find it very difficult to place thems in any setting other than the Rapture.

The first parable is found in Matthew 22:

And when the king came in to see the guests, he saw there a man which had not on a wedding garment: and he saith unto him, Friend, how camest thou in hither not having a wedding garment? And he was speechless. Then said the king to the servants, Bind him hand and foot, and take him away, and cast him into outer darkness, there shall be weeping and gnashing of teeth.

Matthew 22:11-13

It is very difficult for me to put this parable into any other context except the Rapture. The reason is that I simply cannot believe that someone would make it into Heaven and then be cast out of Heaven and thrown into Hell.

The second parable is found in Matthew 25:

Then he which had received the one talent came and said, Lord, I knew thee that thou art an hard man, reaping where thou hast not sown, and gathering where thou hast not strawed: and I was afraid, and went and hid thy talent in the earth: lo, there thou hast that is thine.

His lord answered and said unto him, Thou wicked and slothful servant, thou knewest that I reap where I sowed not, and gather where I have not strawed: thou oughtest therefore to have put my money to the exchangers, and then at my coming I should have received mine own with usury. Take therefore the talent from him, and give it unto him which hath ten talents. For unto every one that hath shall be given, and he shall have abundance: but from him that hath not shall be taken away even that which he hath. And cast ye the unprofitable servant into outer darkness: there shall be weeping and gnashing of teeth. Matthew 25:24-30

BOOM!

Are we really so arrogant as to believe that angels are coming to take us in the Rapture if we are not using our talents for the Kingdom of God? I know this is referring to a talent, or measure, of silver or gold. I find, however, that I do not want the Lord coming back knowing that my commitment to His Lordship is not as close to one hundred percent as I can possibly make it. **BOOM!**

The third parable is found in Matthew 24:

Therefore be ye also ready: for in such an hour as ye think not the Son of man cometh. Who then is a faithful and wise servant, whom his lord hath made ruler over his household, to give them meat in due season? Blessed is that servant, whom his lord when he cometh shall find so doing. Verily I say unto you, That he shall make him ruler over all his goods. But and if that evil servant shall say in his heart, My lord delayeth his coming; and shall begin to smite his fellowservants, and to eat and drink with the drunken; the lord of that servant shall come in a day when he looketh not for him, and in an hour that he is not aware of, and shall cut him asunder, and appoint him his portion with the hypocrites: there shall be weeping and gnashing of teeth. Matthew 24:44-51*

BOOM!

I do not want to ever say,"The Lord delayeth His coming." And I want to make sure that when He comes back, I am not mistreating my fellow servants. I do not want the Lord to have to cut me asunder and appoint my portion with the hypocrites, where there is weeping and gnashing of teeth.

The fourth parable is found in Luke 13:22-30:

And he went through the cities and villages, teaching, and journeying toward Jerusalem. Then said one unto him, Lord, are there few that be saved?
And he said unto them, Strive to enter in at the strait gate: for many, I say unto you, will seek to enter in, and shall not be able. When once the master of the house is risen up, and hath shut to the door, and ye begin to stand without, and to knock at the door, saying, Lord, Lord, open unto us; and he shall answer and say unto you, I know you not whence ye are: then shall ye begin to say, We have eaten and drunk in thy presence, and thou hast taught in our streets. But he shall say, I tell you, I know you not whence ye are; depart from me, all ye workers of iniquity.
There shall be weeping and gnashing of teeth, when ye shall see Abraham, and Isaac, and Jacob, and all the prophets, in the kingdom of God, and you yourselves thrust out. And they shall come from the east, and from the west, and from the north, and from the south, and shall sit down in the kingdom of God. And, behold, there are last which shall be first, and there are first which shall be last.   Luke 13:22-30

One disciple wanted to know if there were going to be many people saved. Jesus responded: *"Strive to be ready. For when the Master of the house rises up and shuts the door, it will then be too late"* (My paraphrase). The people who cannot get in will say they have eaten and drunk in His presence, and He has taught them in their streets. He will respond, *"I do not know you, you workers of iniquity."* The result will be: *"There will be weeping and gnashing of teeth."* **BOOM!**

As I have said with the other parables, I do not know of any other context where this scripture fits except in the Rapture setting. The message of our Lord is: Be Ready and Stay Ready!

If you do not know for sure that your life is ready for the Rapture, cry out to God with all your heart like I did when I was fourteen years of age. Pray that, no matter what happens, God will not let you go to Hell. Ask Jesus Christ to come into your heart and to cleanse you of your sins. Make a commitment to Him, that Jesus Christ, the Son of the living God, will be Lord of your life from this day forward.

Let me put Romans 10:9-10 in my own words:

If you confess with your mouth that Jesus is Lord and believe in your heart that God raised Jesus from the dead, you shall be saved. For with the heart man believes unto righteousness and with the mouth confession is made for salvation.

Claim out loud now with your mouth, using these words: "Thank You, Jesus, for saving my soul! Amen!"

May God bless you with your new commitment to the Lordship of Jesus Christ, and may you walk with Christ with all the commitment you can possibly give Him. If you made that commitment, you now know *How to Be Rapture Ready*!

A PERSONAL MESSAGE FROM
CHARLES BENNETT
HOW I STAY RAPTURE READY

I thought I should share with you how I stay Rapture ready. Years ago, God showed me three things that would help me all the days of my life to not miss the Rapture. They are:

1. **Every day read the Bible and pray.** Me reading the Bible gives God an opportunity to speak to me. Praying to God gives me an opportunity to talk to Him. We need God's wisdom every day, and we need to speak to Him every day to stay in communion with Him.

2. **Go to church at least once every week**. The writer to the Hebrews said (in my own words) for us not to forsake the assembling together of the saints (see Hebrews 10:25). This gives me an opportunity to challenge and be challenged, to exhort and be exhorted and to fellowship with people of like precious faith. It also gives me an opportunity to encourage others and be encouraged by others who love God. No one is an island unto himself. How can I show my love to God if I do not show love for others? Jesus said

that the world would know we are His disciples because we have love for one another (see John 13:35).

3. **Give God ten percent of all my increase, every time I have an increase.** This is the way God has chosen (in my own words):
- To open the windows of heaven.
- To pour out blessings that there is not room enough to receive.
- To rebuke the devil for my sake.
- To make sure my fruit will not drop itself in the field before its time.
- To cause all men to call me blessed (see Malachi 3:10-13).

If you will obey God in your life and faithfully do the things I have outlined here, I believe I will see you in the Rapture. May God bless you!

The Rapture and the Church Is Going Home

The following poem/song was written by my father, C.L. Bennett, in the early 1980s. The wording is exactly what I have been describing to you in this book. It is amazing that I had never seen in the Spirit these concepts until many years after my father had written this. Enjoy!

Verse 1.)

Transportation is provided by the Lord, Insurance underwritten by His Word.
The royal flight to Glory is beginning.
Everyone in gleaming white, leaving on that wedding flight.

Chorus

It's the Rapture, and the Church is going home, going home, going home.
It's the Rapture, and the Church is going home, going home, going home.
It's the Rapture, and the Church is going home.

Verse 2.)

On that grand and glorious flight, Heaven's gates will come in sight.
The gates of pearl will open for us then.
Our Pilot is God's Son. Every battle has been won.

Verse 3.)

That transport will never fail. It will weather every gale.
No passenger will ever suffer loss.
All our cares will flee away on that joyful wedding day!

Verse 4.)

Ever since our second birth, we've been aliens on this Earth.
We're looking for a better place to live.
We seek a city built foursquare and a mansion over there.

Verse 5.)

We will go up in the skies, look the Savior in His eyes,
Standing on that pavilion cloud,
With all our friends who've gone before, leaving for that golden shore.

Verse 6.)

In the distance we shall see the home for you and me.
We'll fly around that holy landing site,
Heaven's armies standing by with their banners flying high.

Verse 7.)

God the Father and His host and the blessed Holy Ghost
Will greet us at the immigration gate.
Praise and worship will begin, joy and gladness never end.

Verse 8.)

The trumpet call is near! Oh, my brother, you must hear,
And turn from all your wicked ways just now.
The time is growing short! All your sins you must abort!

AUTHOR CONTACT

You may contact Pastor Charles Bennett in the following ways:

Founder/Pastor Charles Bennett
Joy Fellowship Worship Center
1001 Perrymont Road
Hopewell, VA 23860

E-mail: Joy-Fellowship@juno.com
Phone: USA (804) 536-5137

Mailing address:
632 Cedar Level Road
Hopewell, VA 23860

COMING SOON: A NEW BOOK BY PASTOR CHARLES BENNETT!

If you enjoyed the insights in this book, you might want to be on the look-out for Pastor Bennett's next book. It is entitled *A Comprehensive Study of Speaking in Other Tongues.* In this book, Pastor Bennett will be discussing the following:

- What language did Adam and Eve speak?
- What really happened at the Tower of Babel?
- Is it possible that Moses understood the language of Heaven?
- Was there a "message in tongues" and "interpretation of tongues" in the Old Testament?
- What really happened on the Day of Pentecost?
- Why is there so much resistance to speaking in tongues if God has chosen to use it?

These and many other subjects will be addressed in the new book:

A COMPREHENSIVE STUDY OF SPEAKING IN OTHER TONGUES!